How do *I feel* about that?

By *Dr. Denise A. Freeman*

Inside the Mind of Your Psychologist

Dr. D.

Copyright © 2024 Dr Denise A. Freeman

All rights reserved.

The characters and events portrayed in this book are fictitious. Any similarity to real persons, living or dead, is coincidental and not intended by the author.

No part of this book may be reproduced, or stored in a retrieval system, or transmitted in any form or by any means, electronic, mechanical, photocopying, recording, or otherwise, without express written permission of the publisher.

ISBN: 9798336742268
ISBN: 9798338093504

Independently published and printed in the United Kingdom.

Navigating Insights:
Your Content Guide

A Special Mention to You for Keeping it Real!	1
A Letter to You	2
Psychological Perspectives	3
My Clinical Perspective	6
A Chirpy Story - Chirpbrain	7
The Why, The What, The How & The Wren	9
In the Beginning	13
Therapy Approach	19
The Therapeutic Process	29
Therapy Boundaries:	
The Unseen Lines of Care	36
Confidentiality	42
Judgement in Therapy	48
Therapeutic Chemistry & Competency	51
Session Location	57
The Virtual Couch:	
Shrinking Distances in Psychotherapy	59
Navigating the Emotional Landscape of Therapy	63
The Secret Life of Therapy:	
What Really Happens Behind Closed Doors	71
Therapeutic ENDINGS	93
Therapy from the Therapist's Chair:	
Personal Impact and Professional Insight	100
Gifts, Gratitude, & Graciousness:	
Navigating the Therapist's Gift Dilemma	112
Beyond the Couch:	
A Therapist's Journey Through Your Healing	117
Things I Say So Often	
They're Probably on a T-Shirt Somewhere	120

A Special Mention to You for Keeping it Real!

*Aneesa P.,
Anisha K, Anna C, Cosmina N, Dal, Dalia, Jamie D,
Olly O Sully, M. Corcoran, Mark T, Pauline I, Rochelle, Sarah D,
Thanuja S.*

*In memory of Michael Acutt,
a man of many miles and warm smiles.*

Dear Patient/Client,

This book is your book. It was written for you, as I know you have questions (and thank you to those who have sent all your questions in) about exactly who you are sharing and entrusting your heart, mind, soul and space with. I hope it answers your questions, as I lift my professional veil to reveal as much of myself as is necessary, so we may continue to focus on you: your emotional recovery, your healing and on your therapeutic journey. May your book, with an insight into the mind of your therapist, solidify and strengthen our dynamic, beneficial connection and our relationship together.

In the pages that follow, you'll notice my personality, and especially my humour, coming through. My light-heartedness and candour are not intended to trivialise, minimise or diminish the significance of your challenges nor the courage and strength that I know it takes, to admit and commit to psychological therapy, with a near stranger.

P.S. As we are evolving all the time, my view and opinions may evolve, but the fundamental aspects of therapeutic safe-keeping and working ethically and responsibly, remain constant.

With metta, because you matter,
Dr. D.

Psychological Perspectives

"Through our sharing, we grow and through our growth we're able to vibrationally affect & raise those around us." – Dr. D

Understanding what any psychologist thinks can be a bit tricky because of the professional boundaries and confidentiality that they must maintain. Psychologists are trained to provide unbiased support and maintain a non-judgmental attitude towards their patients and clients.

If you're curious about your psychologist's thoughts on your progress or treatment, ask them directly: open communication can enhance the therapeutic relationship and provide you with the clarity and reassurance you need.

It might be helpful for you to appreciate that there are some common themes and professional attitudes that many psychologists strive to maintain in their work with patients.

Here are a few insights that might help you understand their perspective:

- **Client-Centered Approach**: Many psychologists use a client-centered approach, meaning they prioritise *your* perspective and *your* experiences. Their primary concern is your well-being and helping you achieve your personal goals.

- **Empathy, Understanding and Compassion**: Most psychologists aim to understand their clients' experiences and feelings with empathy and compassion, and they strive to genuinely care about their clients' well-being and progress.

- **Non-judgmental Attitude**: Psychologists are trained to maintain a non-judgmental attitude. This means they endeavour to create a safe and accepting environment where clients can openly share their thoughts and feelings without fear of being judged.

- **Professional Objectivity**: Psychologists aim to maintain objectivity and neutrality. They focus on helping you understand and manage your thoughts, emotions, and behaviours without imposing their personal judgments.

- **Professional Boundaries**: While psychologists may develop strong emotional connections with their clients, they maintain professional boundaries. This helps ensure that the therapeutic relationship remains focussed on the clients' needs and goals.

- **Respect for Autonomy**: Psychologists respect their clients' autonomy and support their ability to make their own decisions. They provide guidance and support but ultimately recognise that clients have the right to choose their paths.

- **Confidentiality and Trust**: Maintaining confidentiality is a cornerstone of the therapeutic relationship. Psychologists understand the importance of trust and go to great lengths to protect their clients' privacy.

- **Commitment to Ethical Practice**: Psychologists adhere to ethical guidelines and standards set by professional organisations. This includes respecting clients' dignity, avoiding conflicts of interest, and continually seeking to improve their professional competence.

- **Cultural Sensitivity**: Psychologists recognise and respect the diverse cultural backgrounds of their clients. They strive to be culturally sensitive and to understand how cultural factors influence clients' experiences and perspectives.

- **Patience and Persistence**: Psychological change often takes time, and progress can be slow and non-linear. Psychologists understand this, and they are patient and persistent in supporting their clients through setbacks and challenges.

- **Genuine Interest in Human Behaviour**: Many psychologists have a deep interest in understanding human behaviour and mental processes. This curiosity drives their work and helps them stay engaged and motivated to help their clients.

- **Collaborative Approach**: Psychologists often view the therapeutic process as a collaborative effort between themselves and their clients. They work together to identify goals, explore issues, and develop strategies for change.

Overall, while psychologists bring their own unique perspectives and personalities to their work, they are generally committed to providing compassionate, ethical, and effective care to their patients and clients.

My Clinical Perspective

As a psychologist, my clinical perspective is shaped by a blend of psychological, philosophical, and spiritual traditions that emphasise the interconnectedness of all beings and the collective impact of individual growth. I advocate for continuous self-improvement and a conscious commitment to the well-being of others, viewing therapy as a space to explore and integrate all aspects of the self.

Growth:
Therapy is a safe space for personal growth, encompassing intellectual, emotional, and spiritual development. Through thoughtful inquiry and open dialogue, we create the mental space necessary for growth, fostering greater awareness, resilience, and the ability to apply what is learned beyond therapy.

Sharing:
Sharing knowledge and experiences through deep, meaningful discussions promotes personal enrichment and collective growth. This reciprocal exchange not only enhances individual understanding but also extends the benefits to others, contributing to a broader impact.

Vibrational Impact:
Your personal energy and state of being can significantly influence those around you. By aligning with higher vibrational states, characterised by positivity and growth, you emit an energy that can uplift and inspire others. The therapeutic space supports this alignment, promoting well-being.

Raising Others:
Personal growth and positivity have a ripple effect, inspiring and elevating those we interact with. By embodying higher vibrational states, our energy and actions become a catalyst for others' growth and well-being, emphasising that positive change begins within and extends outward.

Chirpbrain

In a forest not too far from here, there was a small, wise wren named Dr. Wrenny, known for being the most unbird-brained psychologist in the animal kingdom. Dr. Wrenny possessed a "mindful song"—calm, contemplative, and deeply attuned, able to gently glide from one thought to the next with a serene clarity, always understanding the broader harmony by sensing the subtle notes within each detail.

One day, a chimpanzee named Charlie, who had a "chatty chimpbrain," came to see Dr. Wrenny. Charlie was struggling. His mind was always full of thoughts, analysing every little detail to the point of exhaustion. He couldn't make decisions without second-guessing himself, and it was starting to wear him down.

Charlie slumped in the chair, scratching his head as he explained, "Dr. Wrenny, I can't stop overthinking! I get so caught up in analysing everything that I feel paralysed. How do I get my brain to just... relax?"

Dr. Wrenny tilted her head, chirping softly as she listened. Then she began to speak, her voice light and quick like her thoughts. "Charlie, your 'chimpbrain' is strong, and that's a gift. It allows you to think deeply, solve complex problems, and understand things in a way many others can't. But sometimes, it helps to add a little *chirp* to the chat."

Charlie looked puzzled. "*Chirp*?"

Dr. Wrenny chirped with a glint in her eye. "Imagine your thoughts as a wild river. If the water's too turbulent, you can't see clearly. But if you add mindfulness, you can smooth out the turbulence."

Charlie frowned. "Mindfulness? How does that help?"

Dr. Wrenny fluttered her wings with enthusiasm. "Think of mindfulness as adding a strong study and very cosy raft to your wild river. By taking deep breaths and focusing on the present, you see yourself comfortably solidly nesting on that raft, letting the river flow around you without getting caught up in every ripple."

Charlie tried to stifle a chuckle. "A sturdy and cosy nest raft? That actually sounds pretty relaxing!"

Dr. Wrenny smiled. "Exactly! So, let's practice. I'll guide you through a simple exercise. Picture yourself ensconced on that solid nest raft, floating effortlessly while your thoughts drift by."

Charlie took a several slow deep breath and imagined himself on a cosy raft. To his surprise, the exercise actually worked! His stress started to melt away, and he felt a lot lighter.

A few weeks later, Charlie returned to Dr. Wrenny, grinning from ear to ear. "Dr. Wrenny, I've been floating on my nest raft, and it's fantastic! I even stopped second-guessing whether my bananas should be organised by size or ripeness!"

Dr. Wrenny chirped with delight. "That's wonderful, Charlie! Remember, creating space for a bit of 'chirpbrain' mindfulness to quieten the 'chimpbrain' chatter can turn even the wildest thoughts into a smooth float."

Charlie laughed. "You're right! I'm glad I can now instruct my 'chimpbrain' for when and how I need it, and the rest of the time, give myself permission to bathe in the melodic zenness of my 'chirpbrain'.

With a happy bounce, Charlie left the forest, grateful for the balance he'd found. He knew that by routinely engaging his mindfulness 'chirpbrain', to balance out his busy, chatty 'chimpbrain', he could navigate the deep, spirally and rocky rivers of his inner world, with a chirpy smile.

THE WHY, THE WHAT, THE HOW & THE WREN

"If you don't do anything, nothing happens."- Birgitta T.

A question everyone (my parents included) wonders about, is why I became a Counselling Psychologist.

Why Psychology?
As a child, I was always curious. I was the kid who annoyed my parents with, "but why..?" and grew up annoying my teachers with the same question, "..but why?" (*Not so much has changed there, as I am always in search of answers!*).

I guess it all started with observing my mum and dad as well as my older sisters, and being consciously mindful of my relationship with each. This led me to observe and be aware of myself: I noticed that I enjoyed disentangling and piecing things together and trying to understand the big picture.

I didn't have to ask the question of "why" when I gravitated towards problem-solving work. Putting things (and people) together gave me joy, made me feel useful, and above all else, there was no question, that I enjoyed helping.

Did your childhood have an influence on your career choices?
Definitely. I enjoyed writing poetry and short stories as a child, so I became a Copywriter. I also wanted to solve crimes and become a Detective (Psychologists make good detectives because they always dig deep into motives)! So, I became a Counselling Psychologist who writes (sans cuffs).

What did you study?
I obtained a Marketing diploma from the Chartered Institute of Marketing (CIM) in Malaysia. This was followed by undergraduate studies in Sociology & Psychology in North Carolina, then an MSc in Psychology at University of East London, followed by a scholarship for a Doctoral Degree in Counselling Psychology from the University of Roehampton, UK.

How many careers have you had?
My first career in my early 20s was in advertising, where I trained as a Copywriter in Malaysia. I later worked as a Creative Director in broadcasting. I also taught advertising and marketing at a university in Malaysia and later in England. I worked as a freelance Copywriter in Finland, whilst conducting cultural and adaptation workshops for a training firm there. I have run a below-the-line advertising agency in Romania whilst organising events for several international hotels at the same time. And, I worked on two self-published music albums in The Netherlands.

In my 40s, I obtained a Doctoral Degree in Counselling Psychology in England, where I now practice. I founded Newus Clinic working with a team of brilliant specialists in the field of psychology and coaching.

I am also an author, presenter, composer and am currently Director and Co-Founder of Louden Limited - more on that later!

Why did you change your career?
When I was in advertising, I enjoyed the use of psychographics in the industry. Around the same time in the 90s, I had a taste of volunteering as a counsellor helping juvenile delinquents and enjoyed it. The catalyst for my shift in careers was a life-changing course with Tony Robbins, which became the impetus for self-discovery and extensive personal development.

How have your life experiences played a role in your work as a Counselling Psychologist?
Working with different cultures and in different countries for many years has definitely brought more to the therapeutic table. It has taught me to be more understanding, patient, flexible, empathetic and respectful of our different identities, mores and belief systems. These experiences have taught me how to respect differences and embrace similarities.

My childhood has also played a role in the shaping and understanding of relationships: my relationship with myself and the world around me.

What did you learn about yourself?
That I had carried limiting-self beliefs, which had impacted my identity, life choices, relationships and my view of the world around me. I am still unpacking my emotional DNA and trying to understand how my thinking plays a role in my thinking!

How do you see yourself in the role of a psychologist?
I am a problem solver! But I believe that roles are just what we wear to negotiate the surface of our conscious reality. The question is, who are we without our roles, titles, jobs, cars, houses etc?

So who are we without our roles, titles, jobs, cars, houses etc?
Students.

What are your strengths as a practitioner?
I am able to have a special and genuine relationship with each of you, because I experience each person and each problem, as unique.

What are your strengths as a person?
My creativity and curiosity, my problem-solving nature, empathy, can-do approach and desire to self-improve and learn.

What are your weaknesses?
There are too many to mention! However, when it comes to clinical work, I do not profess to be able to work with all challenges or concerns. I will at first try but as soon as I realise that you (and I) need more help, I will not hesitate to reach out to someone who can. I still make errors therapeutically but do learn from them!

What does the work you do teach you about people?
That we suffer in different ways. We suffer in silence for too long. And we do not have to go the course alone.

Also, I am constantly amazed by one's strength, courage, resilience, determination, growth and the desire to keep on helping oneself and never giving up. This is truly admirable.

Where does the 'Wren' come into 'the why', 'the what', and 'the how' of becoming a psychologist?
Wrens are known for their keen observational skills. They are always alert, watching their surroundings for both food and potential threats. Just like the wren, I'd say I possess strong observational skills to notice subtle cues in your behaviour, body language, speech patterns and change in personal energy. These observations help in understanding the underlying concerns, your feelings and thoughts as well as helping in the forming of psychological assessments and formulations.

IN THE BEGINNING

What's on your mind when you first speak to a potential client?
Hello!

What's on your mind when you first start talking?
I hope we are a good fit together.

What's the next thing on your mind, if we are a good fit together?
Helloooooo!!

What does being 'a good fit mean?'
It means that we gel/jive therapeutically. That we have therapeutic chemistry. That my competency and skill-set match your presenting challenge(s) and I am able to help. It also means that you feel at ease with me as your practitioner.

Think of it as finding the exact key you need, that will unlock the door, or finding the long-lost piece of the puzzle that will enable you to see the big picture.

What is therapy about?
You!

What do you do? Can you put it simply?
I listen. I feel. I understand. I sense. I ask a lot of (tough) questions.

What do you tell your clients about the nature of talking, in talk therapy?
If I say something that makes you feel uncomfortable, I hope you feel comfortable enough to share it and work through it, together.

What can you offer me psychologically?
A view.

What criteria should I have with (you as) my therapist?
If you do not feel safe with me, run!
If you do not feel I am competent, run!
If you do not feel there is therapeutic chemistry, run!
But do not run away from your problems.

What is the main intention you have in therapy?
I like to always leave you feeling better than when you came in 50 minutes earlier or 5 months earlier. I know I cannot control how you feel and I do not want to make it *my* agenda, because it would be unnatural. You set the intention when you come to therapy and that becomes my intention too. At least, that's the intention!

What else can you offer me psychologically?
Peace of mind. Lightness of the spirit. And sometimes, silence for the soul!

Is this where we solve all my problems?
Define 'problem'.

Is this where we solve all my problems?
I don't solve problems because I don't see problems.

How do I know you can help me?
Therapy is not just about me helping you. It is actually about you and I, engaging, discovering, co-constructing, sharing ideas, questioning, exchanging perspectives and knowledge, and meaning-making. In Uni they just called it "intersubjectively". We explore topics together and co-construct a way forward to obtain clarity and closure..

Can you solve my problems?
Only you can.

What does a positive connection with a therapist look like?

- **Genuine Engagement**: They show genuine interest in your thoughts and feelings, ask meaningful questions, and seem emotionally invested in your well-being. **For example**: Your therapist asks follow-up questions about your hobbies or interests and remembers details from past sessions, showing they are invested in understanding you better.

- **Consistency and Reliability**: They are consistently punctual, respectful, and attentive during sessions, indicating they value your time and your therapeutic relationship. **For example**: They are consistently on time for your sessions and inform you promptly if they need to reschedule. They also prepare for your sessions thoughtfully, addressing previous discussions or progress.

- **Encouragement and Support**: They offer encouragement and validate your experiences, helping you build confidence and self-worth. **For example**: When you share a personal achievement or progress, your therapist offers heartfelt congratulations and positive reinforcement, acknowledging your hard work and growth.

- **Active Listening**: They actively listen and reflect on what you say, showing that they truly understand and care about your perspective. **For example**: They make eye contact, nod, and provide reflections or summaries of what you've shared to ensure they've understood you correctly. They might say, "It sounds like you're feeling overwhelmed by the recent changes at work".

- **Warmth and Empathy**: They exhibit warmth, empathy, and a non-judgmental attitude, making you feel understood and valued. **For example**: They respond to your emotional experiences with compassion, such as saying, "I can imagine how difficult that must have been for you. It's completely understandable to feel this way".

How long is a session?
50 minutes.

What's the shortest time you will see a client for?
50 minutes.

I've agreed to therapy what else do I need to do?
Show up.

I'm in therapy what else do I need to do?
Reflect. Process. Put new thoughts or new beliefs into action. In your own time.

What are my responsibilities as a client?
- To work with me as your psychologist as reasonably requested;
- Be Honest: You're not there to win an Oscar for Best Performance in a Therapy Session. Tell the truth, even if it's as mundane as "I spent three hours watching cat videos and felt oddly fulfilled."
- Engage: Don't just nod and say "uh-huh." This isn't a podcast you're half-listening to. Engage with the process, ask questions, challenge ideas, and maybe even laugh at the absurdity of human behaviour.
- To work with your primary care provider as reasonably requested, including with any medication plan they have prescribed to you;
- To work with our cancellation and notification policies, including giving sufficient notice if you cannot attend an appointment;
- To provide, in a timely manner, any information required, including information regarding your medical records or prescribed medications;

- To pay any invoice provided to you within the specified time.
- After sessions, think about what was discussed. Did something click? Did something annoy you? These reactions are gold in therapy.
- Communicate Issues: If something isn't working, if you feel stuck, or if you're not vibing with your therapist, speak up. Therapy should feel like a journey you're somewhat excited about, not a chore.
- And yes, to show up.

Do you really care?
Yes, I really and genuinely care. And I hope you will get a sense of that when we meet every time.

What should I absolutely not say or do in therapy?
Maintaining a respectful and productive therapeutic relationship involves a few important observations and boundaries:

- Avoid Lying or Exaggerating: Honesty is crucial in therapy. While it might be tempting to embellish or omit details, doing so can hinder progress.
- Don't Expect Friendship: While a therapeutic relationship can be warm, it's not the same as friendship. Avoid seeking personal details (unless you find it here) about your therapist's life or trying to meet outside of sessions.
- Respect Boundaries: Don't push for sessions outside of agreed times or contact your therapist excessively between sessions unless it's an emergency.
- Avoid Aggressive or Abusive Behaviour: This includes verbal attacks, threats, or any form of physical aggression. Therapy is a safe space for both parties.

- Don't Demand Immediate Solutions: Therapy often requires time. Demanding quick fixes or getting impatient can lead to frustration for both you and your therapist.
- Refrain from Making Promises You Can't Keep: If you agree to try certain techniques or changes, follow through. Consistently not doing so can undermine the therapy.
- Avoid Constant Topic Changes: If you jump from one issue to another without fully exploring any, it can make it hard to address underlying issues effectively.
- Don't Ignore Feedback: If your therapist gives you feedback, even if it's hard to hear, dismissing it without consideration can stall progress.
- Avoid Over-dependency: While it's okay to rely on therapy, becoming overly dependent to the point where you can't make decisions without your therapist's input might not be healthy.
- Don't Bring Gifts or Personal Items: Bringing gifts can blur professional boundaries.
- Avoid Discussing Other Clients: Respect confidentiality. Don't ask about or discuss other clients you may have referred, even if you think you know them.
- Don't Expect Your Therapist to Agree with Everything: Therapy isn't about validation but exploration and growth. Expecting constant agreement can limit your therapeutic journey.

The Approach

What is your approach in therapy like?
Integrative.

The Humanistic Hug: I'm like the warm, fuzzy blanket of therapy. I believe everyone's got a little spark of potential, just waiting to be fanned into a flame. I'm not here to tell people they're broken; I'm here to remind them they're a masterpiece in progress. Carl Rogers would be proud, nodding from the great beyond, "Yes, yes, let them be themselves!"

The Psychodynamic Peek: I'm not afraid to dive into the past, like a detective in a time machine. "Let's see what's lurking in the shadows of your psyche," I might say, with a magnifying glass in hand. Freud's ghost probably whispers in my ear, "Tell them about their mother issues!"

The Person-Centered Playpen: Here, I create a space where people can just be. No masks, no pretences. It's like saying, "Come in, take off your shoes, and be yourself. Here, we don't judge; we just grow." It's the therapeutic equivalent of a spa day for the soul.

The CBT Challenge: I'm also the coach who says, "Let's get those thoughts in shape!" I challenge those pesky, negative thoughts like a personal trainer challenges a client to do one more push-up. "Is that thought really helping you? Let's bench press it!"

The Comfortable Pace: I'm not rushing anyone to the finish line of mental health. It's more like a leisurely walk in the park, where I might stop to smell the roses or discuss why the roses make you feel a certain way. "We'll get there when we get there, and we'll enjoy the journey."

So, in essence, my approach is like hosting a mental health festival where everyone's invited, and every booth offers something different, but all with the same goal: to help you find your path to self-actualisation, one laugh, one tear, and one "aha!" moment at a time. This is called integrative therapy, and it tastes likes this:

The Integrative Ice Cream Sundae - I don't just serve one flavour of therapy. Oh no, I'm the therapist who says, "Why choose when you can have all the toppings?" I mix and match like a barista at a hipster coffee shop, but instead of coffee, it's therapy. A bit of Freud here, a sprinkle of Rogers there, and a hefty scoop of CBT on top. "How do you like your therapy? With or without the existential sprinkles?"

Does your approach vary from other therapists?
Although I've worked with only three different therapists, which is a limited sample, I believe that my approach and style, combined with my empathetic nature, problem-solving abilities, and professional intuition, facilitate a deep connection in therapy. Each therapist contributes their own personality to the therapeutic process, and this, along with their chosen methods, creates a unique experience for each client.

How different do you think you are to other therapists?
As a psychologist, my working approach is to provide you with insight into your own psychology and making sense and meaning of some of its (manufactured) contents. I am goal driven, solution-focussed and I am able to ask the tough questions (gently)! I feel that my approach is different because I *feel* my work, although I do not see it as work. I care about what I do too.

Do you have a predetermined set of questions you ask each client?
Two questions I tend to ask, "how are you feeling right now" and "what did you process/reflect on, from our last session together?" There are no wrong answers!

Do you ask questions or do you mainly just listen?
During your assessment, I may ask more questions to gain a comprehensive understanding of your needs. As therapy progresses, my questions will be purposeful—aimed at clarifying points, opening up topics for discussion, and facilitating your growth and understanding, always in alignment with the therapeutic goals we've established together.

I understand that, especially at the beginning of therapy and at the start of each session, you may have a lot to express and release, which is completely valid and important. As we move forward, you'll be doing most of the talking, while I listen actively and chime in when needed. Think of it as you being the lead vocalist, and I'm just the backup vocals, chirping in when it counts!

Do you direct your sessions?
Not quite—I'm like a co-pilot. I keep your goals in mind, but the direction is all yours. My approach is more of a collaborative journey than a guided tour.

Do you control your sessions?
Define control.

Do you control your sessions?
Aren't we controlled enough in life?

Are you empathetic?
Yes, and intuitively so. I feel you and feel my work with you.

Do you also use your intuition when you work?
I may use my felt-sense, or professional intuition when I work with you.

What kind of clients do you attract?
Hopefully those I can help!

How do you beef up your knowledge and keep up-to-date?
I read, watch videos, have supervision, have my own therapy, listen to podcasts and do CPDs (Continuing Practice Development), which is a requirement by my professional body.

How do you deal with complicated clients?
Without complicating matters.

How do you deal with complicated clients?
There are no complicated clients, just complicated life experiences.

How do you deal with complicated clients?
Simply.

What is the one thing you often tell your clients?
If I speak too fast, tell me quickly!

What is the one thing you often tell your clients?
If I ask a question that makes you squirm, just let me know. I promise, my questions are like my jokes—awkward but well-intentioned!

What do you often tell your clients?
If you cannot answer a question, it's ok, we can always come back to it (or not) later.

Can therapy become an obsession?
Yes, therapy can potentially become an obsession if it's used as a way to avoid dealing with life's challenges directly or if it starts to overshadow other aspects of life. Ideally, therapy is a tool for growth and self-discovery, not a constant focus. If you find yourself preoccupied with it to the point where it interferes with your daily functioning, it might be worth discussing this, to ensure it's serving your well-being in a balanced way.

What do you think of medication?

When it comes to medication, its effectiveness really depends on the specific issue at hand. I usually start by getting a clear picture of your needs before considering medication. While I don't prescribe meds myself, I can refer you to a general practitioner or psychiatrist if needed. Just a heads-up: if medication is recommended and you choose not to follow through, I may have to reconsider continuing therapy due to ethical and safety reasons. It's all about ensuring you're getting the best and safest care possible.

1. **Treatment Effectiveness**
   - **Comprehensive Treatment Plan:** For certain mental health conditions, particularly severe ones like schizophrenia, bipolar disorder, or major depressive disorder, medication is often a crucial component of the treatment plan. If you refuse medication, I may feel that I cannot effectively help you, as therapy alone may not be sufficient.
   - **Limited Progress:** If I believe that the lack of medication is significantly hindering progress in therapy, I might feel that continuing treatment under these circumstances is not beneficial for you. Without the necessary biochemical balance that medication can provide, therapy might not yield the desired outcomes.

2. **Ethical Consideration**
   - **Do No Harm:** Psychologists adhere to ethical guidelines that emphasise "do no harm". If refusing medication could lead to a worsening of your condition or pose a risk to your well-being, I might feel ethically obligated to insist on medication as part of the treatment plan.
   - **Informed Consent and Treatment Refusal:** While you, as the client/patient have the right to refuse treatment, including

medication, psychologists also have the right to set boundaries for the conditions under which they can work effectively. If you refuse a recommended and essential part of the treatment, it might compromise my ability to provide ethical and effective care.

3. **Safety Concerns**
   - **Patient Safety:** In cases where not taking medication could lead to dangerous behaviour, such as self-harm, suicide, or violence, I might refuse to treat you, as I cannot ensure your safety through therapy alone.
   - **Public Safety:** If you pose a potential threat to others without medication (e.g., in cases of severe psychosis), I might be unwilling to continue treatment unless you agree to take the necessary medication to manage these risks.

4. **Professional Responsibility**
   - **Scope of Practice:** Psychologists are not medical doctors and typically do not prescribe medication, but they often work in conjunction with psychiatrists or other medical professionals who do. If you refuse to follow the comprehensive treatment plan that includes medication, I might feel that my professional responsibility requires that I refer you to another provider who can better address your needs.
   - **Legal Liability:** In some cases, if you were to harm yourself or others due to a refusal to take prescribed medication, I could potentially face legal and professional repercussions. To avoid such liability, I may refuse to treat you under these conditions.

5. **Patient Autonomy vs. Professional Judgment**
   - **Balancing Act:** While as a psychologist, I respect client/patient autonomy, there are limits. If a psychologist believes that a patient's refusal of medication is significantly detrimental to their health or safety, they might feel it is in the patient's best interest to refuse treatment unless the patient is willing to adhere to the full treatment plan.

In summary, if you're skipping your prescribed medication, I might have to pass on treating you. It's not about being a hard-nose; it's just that without the medication, my therapy could be like trying to drive a car with a flat tire — ineffective and a bit of a hazard!

What if I do not want medication?
I might have to step back from providing therapy if you've been recommended medication by your psychiatrist or doctor, and you decide against taking it. As a psychologist, I'm bound by the limits of what I'm trained to do. If I believe that your treatment would be better served with medication, or if your situation is too complex for therapy alone, I might suggest we pause or reconsider our sessions. This isn't about not wanting to help, but about making sure you get the kind of help that's most likely to work for you.

How do you know if we have met my therapeutic goals?
When you/we decide it's time to end therapy.

I want solutions now! Can you not do this?
I'm concerned when you seek a quick fix in therapy. Even quick fixes need strong glue. What will be the 'glue' that connects us to your story and keeps us engaged in the journey of meaningful discovery throughout the therapeutic process?

How quick can you get me out of here?
Well, I don't do shortcuts, but I can be tactical and solutions-focussed. Think of it as a road trip—we'll take the fastest route we can, but if there's traffic (going a long way back), we might need to take the scenic path. Healing takes time, but I'll keep us moving forward with a solution-focused approach and keeping an eye on our goals. Just don't expect a drive-thru version of therapy.

Can we have just one session?
If I had a quick-fix button, I'd be using it myself—therapy's more of a 'slow cooker' than a 'microwave'!

Can you describe how a solution-focussed approach works?
This approach emphasises finding solutions to your challenges rather than focussing extensively on the challenges themselves, and rather than dwelling on past problems or extensive analysis of issues. This approach is future-oriented and goal-directed, helping you identify and leverage your strengths to create positive changes in your life. It may not be suitable for everyone, particularly clients who need to explore deep-seated issues or trauma. It might also be less effective for individuals who are not clear about their goals or who are looking for a more exploratory type of therapy.

Would you be able to help me with my trauma?
In theory, yes. However, adopting a solution-focussed approach, may not be as useful or helpful as trauma-focussed therapies that prioritise the processing of traumatic memories, understanding their impact, and developing coping mechanisms. The latter approach is generally more effective for individuals dealing with trauma.

Here are key reasons why the solution-focused approach may be ineffective for trauma survivors and I will instead use an integrative approach to help:

- **Underemphasis on Trauma History:** The approach focuses on immediate goals and future solutions, often neglecting the need to address and process past trauma, which is crucial for many survivors' healing.

- **Risk of Re-traumatisation:** By focusing on the future, this approach may overlook the need for careful trauma exploration, potentially leading to re-traumatisation or worsening of symptoms.

- **Neglect of Underlying Issues:** The brief nature of this approach may miss deep psychological issues tied to trauma, which are essential for long-term recovery.

- **Inadequate for Severe Trauma Symptoms:** For those with severe symptoms like PTSD or dissociation, more intensive and specialised interventions are often necessary, which the solution-focused approach may not provide.

- **Potential for Superficial Solutions:** Emphasising quick solutions can lead to temporary fixes that don't address the trauma's root causes, leaving issues unresolved and potentially resurfacing later.

- **Lack of Emotional Processing:** Trauma recovery often requires processing difficult emotions, which this approach may not adequately support.

How do you work with trauma?
It's a bit like guiding someone through a dense forest—you might feel lost at first, but I'm here to help you navigate the rough terrain. We'll take it one step at a time, sometimes doubling back, but always moving forward. It's not about erasing the past, but about finding a path to healing and resilience. I work with integrative therapy.

Can I choose what kind of psychological modality or approach I would prefer?
Sure, but let's first discuss why you think a particular approach may work better for you. And based on your psychological formulation, would you be happy for me to recommend what approach may also work for you, based on my professional experience?

Can I leave it up to you, to decide what kind of psychological modality or approach would work for me?
Sure. We can always revisit the approach when we do our mid-way check-in or at any time you wish to have a review.

How will we know if we haven't met our therapeutic goals?
We'll both recognise it, and when the time is right, we'll make the decision together to conclude therapy, if necessary.

How long should I stay in therapy?
As long as is required and necessary or when your concerns are resolved or when you feel better. This could be any length of time. Think of therapy like going to the gym. It'll take as long as it takes, to get those mental muscles in shape.

How long should I stay in therapy?
Until you've figured out all the answers to life, the universe, and everything. But since that might take a while, let's aim for when you can say, "I've got this", more often than "I need to talk about this".

The Therapeutic Process

How does therapy work?
You come in, you talk about an issue on your mind, I listen, we work on the issues together, and when you feel better, you leave!

What is the therapeutic journey like?
The journey through therapy encompasses a spectrum of experiences that help you delve into your thoughts, emotions, and behaviours with the guidance of a professional. It involves:

- Exploration: Uncovering the layers of your psyche, like an archaeologist of the self, digging through memories, feelings, and patterns.

- Understanding: Gaining insights into why you think or react in certain ways, often connecting past experiences with present behaviours.

- Skill Development: Learning new coping strategies, communication skills, or ways to manage stress and anxiety.

- Emotional Processing: Working through grief, anger, joy, or any emotion that's been bottled up or misunderstood.

- Goal Setting: Identifying what you want to achieve from therapy, whether it's better relationships, self-esteem, or managing a specific issue like addiction or depression.

- Reflection: Regularly looking back at progress, celebrating small victories, and adjusting the therapeutic approach as needed.

- Support: Having a safe space to express yourself without judgment, where your therapist acts as a mirror, reflecting back your strengths and areas for growth.

- Change: Gradually shifting perspectives, behaviours, or life choices, moving towards a more fulfilling life.

Therapy is not just about solving problems but about understanding oneself more deeply, fostering growth, and sometimes, simply finding someone who listens intently to your story.

I have been told that therapy can set you back?
Psychological therapy can be challenging initially, for several reasons:

1. **Emotional Intensity**: Therapy often involves exploring deep-seated emotions and past traumas, which can be painful and difficult to face.
2. **Self-Reflection**: The process requires a high level of self-awareness, authenticity and honesty, which at first can be uncomfortable and confronting.
3. **Behavioural Changes**: Implementing new coping strategies and changing long-standing patterns of behaviour that are hard-wired can be difficult and require persistent effort until the new behaviour becomes the new habit.
4. **Vulnerability**: Opening up to a therapist involves a degree of vulnerability and trust, which can be hard for many people.
5. **Time and Patience**: Progress in therapy is often gradual, requiring time, patience, and consistent work outside of sessions.

Despite these initial challenges, you will find therapy to be a profoundly rewarding and transformative experience, offering significant benefits for your mental health and overall well-being.

Can I take notes on my phone while in therapy?
Absolutely.

Can I check my phone while in therapy?
What would you be checking for?

Is therapy hard?
Therapy is a process of discovery, a journey into the deep layered self, where you find not only the root of pain and the cause of your certain ways of unhealthy thinking and being, but also the seeds of healing and growth. It is a courageous act of confronting the past, embracing the present, and having the right tools to chisel the future.

Can I check my phone while in therapy?
Sure, and I am also happy to work on any phone addiction issue you have ;-)

Can I take notes in therapy?
Do feel free to take notes, and doodle if it helps.

But don't you keep notes?
Not after the first few sessions. I have scribbles/jottings on my notepad during sessions which I shred as soon as the session is completed that day. Your full name is not on these jottings either.

Can you give me homework?
Five stars to you for wanting to do all you can, for yourself.

Can you give me homework?
I will, if there is a reason to.

Can you give me homework?
Do you want homework?

Do you usually ask a client to do anything for their therapy?
I may leave you with a question at the end of our session to reflect upon for the following week.

What is a psychological formulation?

A psychological formulation is a comprehensive and structured understanding of a person's psychological difficulties or mental health issues. It is developed collaboratively by a psychologist or mental health professional with the individual and is based on psychological theories and research. The formulation goes beyond diagnosis by exploring the underlying causes, contributing factors, and maintaining processes of the individual's problems. Here are the key components typically included in a psychological formulation:

1. **Presenting Issues**: A detailed description of the current problems and symptoms that brought you to therapy.

2. **History**: Relevant background information including developmental history, family dynamics, significant life events, and any previous mental health issues.

3. **Triggering Events**: Identification of recent events or changes that may have triggered the current difficulties.

4. **Predisposing Factors**: Long-standing vulnerabilities such as genetic predispositions, early childhood experiences, and personality traits that may make you more susceptible to psychological problems.

5. **Precipitating Factors**: Immediate factors or stressors that have contributed to the onset of the current difficulties.

6. **Perpetuating Factors**: Ongoing issues or behaviours that maintain the problems, such as maladaptive coping strategies, ongoing stressors, and negative thought patterns.

7. **Protective Factors**: Strengths, resources, and positive aspects of your life that can help in managing or overcoming the problems.

8. **Mechanisms**: The underlying psychological mechanisms that explain how the problems developed and are maintained, often drawing on cognitive-behavioural, psychodynamic, systemic, or other psychological theories.

9. **Treatment Plan**: Based on the formulation, a tailored intervention plan is developed, which may include therapy, medication, lifestyle changes, and other strategies to address the identified issues.

10. **Goals**: Clear, specific, and measurable goals for therapy or treatment, agreed upon by both the therapist and the individual.

A psychological formulation is a dynamic and evolving process, often revisited and revised as therapy progresses and new insights are gained. It aims to provide a coherent narrative that helps you and I understand the problem in a way that guides effective intervention and supports recovery.

Why are psychological formulations tentative?

Every psychologist has a psychological formulation about a client's case and presenting issue(s) after the assessment and at the commencement of therapy. A psychological formulation contains the goals of the therapy, based on what the client issue is, where it originates from, what maintains it, what the behavioural aspects are as a result of the issue, and how the psychologist plans to work with the case. It's the who, what, when, where, why and how of the client and the issue. The formulation is tentative because we discover more things along the way so the 'prognosis' will have to be tweaked or changed.

E.g. You present with concerns about your new job and a lack of confidence, seeking strategies to enhance your self-assurance. You mention that the phrase '*feeling like a fraud*' particularly resonates with

alk about "therapeutic gemstones". What are they?
ften hear me refer to "therapeutic gemstones." These are the key
ts or meaningful takeaways that emerge at the end of each
n. Just like rare gems, these moments are precious—offering
, empowerment, or a fresh perspective. My aim is to ensure that
ave each session feeling enriched, with something valuable to
nto and reflect upon in your journey of growth and healing.

if we never resolve my issue?
alk about why you feel this way.

o not seem to have all the answers to my issues.
hat would that be like for you?

o not seem to have the answers to my issues?
asking the right question?

o you sometimes ask me to summarise our session?
e it is important for us to know what resonated with you in
ssion. It is not a test.

u tell me what will happen to me?
wish I had a crystal ball so I can tell you that everything will be
will be ok and your life will turn out just fine. All we have is
her, in this space to work with, now. Let's revisit the future in
re.

I cannot get my usual time with you in the online diary?
diary can get full if you do not book in early enough. It's the
ou are booking a flight, a room or cinema tickets. So book your
ments ahead.

you, given your recent entry into the workforce. We sta
a tentative psychodynamic formulation to understand

Through a deeper psychodynamic exploration, we un
high school, you experienced bullying and were de
'monofrau' due to the appearance of your eyebrows.
which remains unresolved, has subtly influenced yo
contributes to your current sense of inadequacy at wo
physical appearance and past bullying have no direc
work competencies or skills, they have significantly i
perception.

We recognise that 'feeling like a fraud' may serve as
entry point for addressing underlying issues tha
suppressed trauma directly. The unresolved trau
bullying and the associated negative self-image ha
to your own current feelings of fraudulence, in
addressing but avoiding the issue.

The revised psychodynamic formulation incorpo
trauma to help us address these deep-seated i
through the unresolved trauma, we can begin
perception. Once these underlying issues are pro
address any remaining concerns related to
confidence and competence.

Can I challenge your interpretations and interve
You must and should! The therapist doesn't have
aren't always right either. Our understandi
reformulations build on the knowledge of you a
about sense-making and meaning-making. We d

Therapy Boundaries:
The Unseen Lines of Care

What are your therapeutic boundaries?
Imagine you're stepping into a magical, yet very professional, realm where the rules are like invisible fences around a garden of healing. These are therapeutic boundaries - not the kind that keep you out, but the kind that make sure your journey through therapy is as safe, effective, and ethical as possible.

- Time: Think of your therapy session like a favourite TV show. It has a start and an end time. Showing up late or wanting to stay longer might be like changing the channel in the middle of a plot twist. It's not just about the clock; it's about respecting the structure that helps therapy work.

- Fees: This isn't just about the money; it's about understanding that therapy, like any craft, has its costs. It's like knowing the price of your favourite coffee before you order. Some therapists might be flexible, but knowing the 'menu' upfront helps everyone.

- Contact Between Sessions: Imagine if your therapist was like a friend who texts you all the time. That would blur the lines, right? Boundaries here ensure that your therapist is there for your therapy, not for casual chats. But, if you're in crisis, they'll have a protocol for that too.

- In-Session Behaviour: Ever been to a party where someone just helps themselves to the fridge? In therapy, asking for a glass of water might seem trivial, but some therapists might see it as stepping into their personal space. Others might have a jug ready, seeing it as part of creating a comfortable environment. It all depends on the kind of psychological modality they practice.

These boundaries are not just rules; they're an integral part of your therapeutic contract, often unspoken but essential. They ensure that your therapist remains professional, ethical, and focused on your growth, not on being a friend or critic outside the session.

Additional notes for my practice:
- Cancellation Policy: I require 48 hours' notice for cancellations. If you miss a session, it is considered lost, even if you've paid for it. You can amend or cancel a session within this 48-hour window using the booking confirmation you received initially.
- Read More: For a detailed understanding, please review my terms online. I aim to keep this engaging, but the details might make you yawn if I delve too deep here!

Remember, these boundaries are designed to make your therapeutic journey smoother, safer, and more focused on your healing than on logistical or social distractions.

Do we have a kind of relationship?
The Setup: You walk into my office, and I'm not just any therapist; I'm the Chief of Boundary Maintenance. My job? To make sure our relationship has more boundaries than a football field! I believe all relationships should have boundaries.

Is this a kind of a relationship?
Yes, a one-sided one. You tell me as much as you are able to about yourself and I tell you nothing of myself. Yet, I bring all of myself to therapy, to engage with you.

What type of relationship is this?
This is a **therapeutic relationship,** where you and your therapist team up to work on whatever's on your mind. Think of it as a safe and

supportive partnership, where your therapist is like a guide, helping you navigate through your thoughts and feelings. They set some ground rules—kind of like the guidelines for a great adventure—to keep things comfortable and professional. With clear boundaries in place, you can focus on making progress while your therapist makes sure everything stays on track!

Can I reach you whenever I need to?
Well, your sessions are like a VIP concert—there's a specific time and date just for you! I don't do surprise pop-up shows outside my usual clinic hours, but feel free to call and see if I can make room, if something urgent comes up. If I'm not available, think of a psychological helpline as the 24/7 drive-thru of support—always open when you need a quick chat!

What if we're about to hit on something big, but it's time to end or session?
Well, that's when I say, "To be continued!" Therapy cliff-hangers are just like your favourite TV show—you'll have to tune in next week to find out what happens next! Don't worry, I'll keep the plot twist safe until our next episode.

What if I start crying just as we're about to end—will you automatically cut off and end our time?
Well, I don't have an off switch, so if the tears start flowing right at the end, I won't just hit pause and leave you hanging. If I've got some extra time, I'll hang around like an encore at a concert—because sometimes, the big emotional moments deserve a little extra stage time.

If it is my first session with you and I am late because I am disoriented and am anxious, can we extend our time together?
If you find yourself running late for our first session because those pesky nerves got the best of you, no worries! Here's how we'll handle it:

- **I Get It**: Showing up to therapy for the first time can be a bit nerve-wracking, and sometimes anxiety likes to play tricks with the clock.

- **Session Time**: I aim to stick to our scheduled time, but I totally understand that life—and nerves—can get in the way.

- **A Little Wiggle Room**: I'll do my best to accommodate you if you're running late, but there are some practical limits.

- **15-Minute Grace Period**: I'll wait for you up to 15 minutes after our start time. If you're not there by then, I'll assume you've decided to give anxiety the day off.

- **Missed Session**: If you don't make it, I'll shoot you an email to let you know the session is considered missed (even if it's already paid for).

- **Looking Ahead**: If we can't squeeze in extra time this session, no sweat! There's always next week, and we can tackle that punctuality anxiety together. This way, we keep things on track while also giving a nod to the real challenges of getting to therapy on time.

Do you talk about yourself in therapy?
Keep reading!

Can I ask you questions about yourself in therapy?
The session is about you?

Can I ask you about you?
Well, you could, but I'm like a side character in your movie—this session is all about you! So, let's keep the spotlight where it belongs: on your story, not my IMDB page!

Can you remind me to talk about my confidence issues with men?
I am sorry, you cannot ask me to remind you to bring up a subject matter next week. I am not your PA.

Can you remind me to talk about XYZ next week?
Can you remind you?

I am going away, should I tell you?
Talk to me before you plan to be away from therapy. This helps me understand where you are (at) therapeutically and helps me plan my diary.

Can you read the email I sent you? I want to check if you think I should send this to my boss.
I would prefer you read it to me in therapy.

Do you talk about yourself in therapy?
Sometimes I may choose to share my most intimate stories with you, but make no mistake: it is not to detract from the importance or processing of your story, suffering or challenges. We are all part of the same human fabric that bonds us, and shared stories can at times help tie loose threads.

Will you speak to my partner about going to therapy?
I work on the premise that you cannot force a person to go to therapy if they are not ready. They have to reach out to a therapist (not yours) on their own.

Does a therapeutic relationship ever have an end?
You and I have a kind of relationship. There is a beginning, a middle and an ending. Hopefully a happy ending. Having said that, a therapeutic relationship can end, but not before we've wrapped up every plot twist and character development. It's like a long-running TV

series—sometimes there's a finale, but you never know if there's going to be a surprise sequel.

Does a therapeutic relationship ever have an end?
Only if the therapist finally figures out how to stop the clock, or you find the ultimate life hack! Spoiler alert: it's usually more about finding closure than closing credits.

Do you offer concessions?
No. But I do know colleagues who will.

Confidentiality

Is therapy confidential?
Yes. Ensuring confidentiality is a cornerstone of ethical practice in psychology. Psychologists are bound by professional codes of conduct. This means that psychologists must follow specific ethical guidelines and standards set by professional organisations, such as the British Psychological Society (BPS) or the American Psychological Association (APA) or similar bodies in other countries. These codes of conduct outline how psychologists should behave in their professional roles, including how they treat clients, maintain confidentiality, avoid conflicts of interest, and ensure their practice is ethical, respectful, and in the best interests of those they serve. Violating these codes can result in disciplinary action, including the loss of their license to practice and suspension of memberships.

In some circumstances, I may have an ethical and legal obligation to disclose your confidential information to third parties. This includes any situation where I may be concerned that not disclosing it could:
- Seriously endanger your own welfare or that of another; and/or
- Seriously endanger the community; and/or
- Cause a serious threat to me, as your psychologist.

How can you ensure confidentiality?

1. **Informed Consent**
   - **Explanation of Confidentiality:** At the outset of therapy, I will clearly explain the limits of confidentiality to you, including the circumstances under which it might be legally or ethically broken (e.g., imminent harm to self or others, child abuse, or court orders).

- **Written Consent:** You will sign a therapy agreement acknowledging that you understand these limits and the psychologist's responsibility to maintain confidentiality.

2. Secure Record Keeping

- **Physical Records:** Paper records are stored in locked cabinets in a secure location, accessible only to authorised personnel.
- **Electronic Records:** Digital records are password-protected and encrypted on secure platforms for storage and transmission of information utilises only security protocols.
- **Access Control:** Only those who are authorised (e.g., the psychologist and any support staff with a legitimate need) should have access to your records.

3. Confidential Communication

- **Private Sessions:** Ensure that therapy sessions are conducted in a private space where conversations cannot be overheard.
- **Secure Communication Channels:** Usage of secure and encrypted methods for any electronic communication with you (e.g., email, text messages). I eschew the discussing of sensitive information through unsecured means.
- **Anonymity:** When discussing cases for supervision, consultation, or research purposes, I remove any identifying information to protect your identity.

4. Confidentiality Agreements with Support Staff

- **Training:** All support staff (e.g., receptionists, billing personnel) are trained in the ethics and practices of confidentiality and their responsibility to maintain it.
- **Agreements:** Support staff sign confidentiality agreements outlining their duty to protect your information.

5. Handling Legal Requests

- **Legal Consultation:** If a legal request for records is received, I will consult with a lawyer to understand the legal obligations and to ensure that my response as a psychologist is consistent with ethical guidelines.
- **Client Notification:** Whenever possible, inform you about any legal requests for your records before disclosing any information.

6. Ethical and Legal Compliance

- **Professional Standards:** My clinic stays updated on the ethical standards and legal requirements regarding confidentiality in the jurisdiction where we practice.
- **Continuing Education:** I regularly participate in continuing education focussed on confidentiality and ethics to ensure best practices are followed.

7. Handling Emergencies

- **Crisis Situations:** When a client poses an immediate threat to themselves or others, I may need to break confidentiality to prevent harm. However, only the necessary information would be disclosed, and you will be informed of the breach as soon as it is safe to do so.

8. Confidentiality After Death

- **Posthumous Confidentiality:** Respect for confidentiality extends even after your death. Information will only be disclosed if legally required or if you previously provided consent for certain disclosures.

9. **Supervision and Peer Consultation**
    - **Anonymity in Discussion:** When discussing cases for supervision or consultation, unless you have provided explicit consent, I maintain your anonymity by omitting or altering identifying details.

How long will my information remain confidential?
Confidentiality is like the Fort Knox of therapy — it's locked up tight and stays that way, even after therapy ends! There is no time limit to your information being confidential, and it will remain as such long after your death, unless overriding legal or ethical considerations require that it should be broken.

Can I tell you anything?
I am open to hearing everything and anything. No holds barred.

Can I tell you everything?
When you do not share what you should be sharing in therapy, you will still get the best of me, but you will not be getting the most out of your best.

Can I tell you everything?
Please, don't hold back!

Can I tell you everything?
Tell me what you are going to tell me, tell me, then tell me what you told me. Or just tell me.

Do you mention my name and details to your supervisor?
No. I just use your first name or your initials.

Do you talk about me outside therapy?
I do not talk about you to my friends or family. We are not encouraged to do so. I may talk about you in supervision using your initials.

Do you talk about me outside therapy?
I respect our confidentiality.

Do you talk about me to other people, like your friends?
That is a strict No-No! (And my friends only want to talk about themselves).

Can I trust you?
Yes

Can I trust you?
Yes

Can I trust you?
Yes

Can I trust you?
I realise, trust takes time to build. Yes.

Can I trust you?
Would you like to talk about 'trust'?

What if I tell you that I did not like my previous therapist?
You just did! Is this something you would like to unpack in this therapeutic space?

Shall I tell you why I did not like my previous therapist?
Sure, if you feel that it would help me understand your psychological needs better.

I did not like my previous therapist..?
Yes, you did not like your previous therapist because you talked and talked but walked away without solutions. So, you found a solution yourself, and left. Power to you.

Do you have a form for me to fill in and sign? Is it long?
There is a therapy agreement for you to read and fill in but nothing that I hope will cause you more anxiety! The agreement is necessary as it safeguards both you and me.

Judgement in Therapy

Do you judge?
I do not judge, I evaluate.

Do you judge me on how I have attended to my issues?
You have engaged me to help you, there is no judgement. Just curiosity on how you see judgement and if you tend to judge yourself and have the belief that others are judging you. Let's talk about where this 'judgement' has come from?

Do you judge me for not telling you in the beginning that I was having an affair with my boss at work?
You did not tell me you had an affair because you thought I'd judge you. I understand, now let's get to work.

Do you judge your clients?
I'd sooner judge myself rather harshly if I find myself judging my clients!

How do you control your personal judgement with your clients?
In therapy, I focus on providing thoughtful observations and insights rather than personal judgment. My role is to offer guidance based on professional knowledge, and I prefer to frame my input as "in my professional opinion" rather than making judgments.

It's important to note that judgment often involves labelling or rigid beliefs, which can hinder progress. I aim to maintain a flexible and open approach in therapy, allowing for growth and exploration rather than getting stuck in fixed judgments. Just as our understanding of psychological concepts is always evolving, so too is our therapeutic process, which thrives on fluidity and adaptability.

Do you judge your clients?
Judging a client would be like handing down a life sentence for the crime of being vulnerable! Instead, I focus on understanding and supporting you without labels or fixed opinions.

Do you judge?
Judging a client defies why we are both in a space that encourages growth.

You sound like you are judging me?
Being judgy does not and cannot facilitate growth. For both me and my clients.

Are you judging me?
I will let you be the judge of that.

You must see me as ugly and weak?
Actually, I see you as someone who is incredibly brave and resilient. Everyone has their own challenges, and my role is to support and help you recognise your strengths and potential.

Do you have an opinion of me?
No, opinions just keep you in a box. There's time for that (the box).

Do you have an opinion of me?
I do not have an opinion of you. To have one is to make a judgement. I do not judge.

Do you judge what I did in that situation?
I may evaluate a situation but I don't judge you for getting into it.

Did you judge me for having an affair with a married man?
No. I will let you be the judge of that.

Do you get annoyed when you have to go through the same thing with the same person each week?
Never. I have the ability to say the same thing in many different ways with many different examples, mainly because I forget how I put it across to you each time!

Do you think your clients see you unnecessarily?
You might wonder if our sessions are necessary from your perspective. It's important to recognise that necessity can be subjective. What I perceive as essential might differ from your view, and that's perfectly valid. Our focus should remain on your feelings and the objectives we've set for your therapy. What's crucial is aligning with your needs and our shared therapeutic goals, rather than my own judgments of right or wrong.

Therapeutic Chemistry & Competency

What happens if you don't vibe with a client?

"Therapeutic chemistry" refers to the emotional, psychological, and relational "chemistry" or connection between a therapist and a client. This connection, often called the therapeutic alliance or therapeutic relationship, is crucial for the success of therapy.

In simple terms, if we don't vibe, it may be because we're thinking and feeling in different frequencies. That may change over time as we get to know each other. If it doesn't change over time, our relationship may cease and that is ok. Therapeutic chemistry is important because:

Building Trust

- Foundation of Trust: A strong therapeutic chemistry fosters trust between you and I. Trust is essential because it allows you to feel safe, supported and open to sharing your thoughts, feelings and experiences without fear of judgment.
- Encouraging Vulnerability: You are more likely to engage deeply in therapy and be honest about your challenges when you feel a genuine connection with me.

Enhancing Engagement and Commitment

- Motivation to Participate: A positive therapeutic chemistry increases your motivation to engage in the therapy process. When you feel understood and valued, you are more likely to commit to the therapeutic process, attend sessions regularly, and participate actively.
- Adherence to Treatment Plans: Clients who feel a strong connection with their therapist are more likely to follow through with therapeutic interventions and homework assignments.

Facilitating Emotional Healing

- Safe Space for Exploration: A strong therapeutic bond creates a safe and supportive environment where you can explore difficult emotions, confront painful memories, and work through trauma.
- Empathy and Understanding: The therapist's ability to empathise with and understand your experiences plays a significant role in helping you process and heal from emotional wounds.

Improving Outcomes

- Therapeutic Effectiveness: Research consistently shows that the quality of the therapeutic relationship is one of the strongest predictors of positive outcomes in therapy, <u>regardless of the specific therapeutic approach used.</u>
- Client Satisfaction: Clients who experience a strong therapeutic connection are generally more satisfied with their therapy experience and more likely to report positive changes in their mental health.

Facilitating Insight and Growth

- Promoting Self-Reflection: A therapist with whom a client feels a strong connection can guide the client to deeper self-reflection and insight. This process is often essential for personal growth and change.
- Challenging Constructively: When there is good therapeutic chemistry, I am likely to be able to challenge your thoughts and behaviours in a constructive way that leads to growth, rather than causing defensiveness or withdrawal.

Supporting Resilience in Therapy

- Managing Difficult Sessions: Therapeutic chemistry helps you and I navigate difficult sessions, where painful or challenging topics are

addressed. The trust and rapport built through this connection can help you stay engaged even when therapy becomes tough.
- Building Resilience: A strong therapeutic bond can help you build resilience by being a model of a healthy, supportive relationship, which you can internalise and apply in other areas of your life.

Providing a Corrective Emotional Experience

- Healing Relational Wounds: For clients who have experienced difficult or traumatic relationships in the past, a strong therapeutic relationship can serve as a corrective emotional experience, helping you to develop healthier relational patterns.
- Modelling Positive Relationships: The therapeutic relationship can serve as a model for other relationships in your life, demonstrating how trust, empathy, and mutual respect can foster healthy connections.

Facilitating Change

- **Supporting Behaviour Change:** Therapeutic chemistry creates a conducive environment for you to experiment with new behaviours and thought patterns. The support and encouragement from a trusted therapist can make it easier for you to take risks and make positive changes.
- Empowering you: When you feel understood and supported by your therapist, you may feel empowered to make changes in your life that aligns with your values and goals.

In summary, therapeutic chemistry is important because it creates the foundation for a successful therapy experience, enabling trust, engagement, emotional healing, and lasting change.

How do you treat patients that you might not be fond of?
With care.

How do you treat patients that you might not be fond of?
I work on my feelings in supervision.

How do you treat patients that you might not be fond of?
When I encounter a client who might challenge me personally, I focus on understanding what aspects are triggering those feelings. I then reflect on whether there's something I need to address in myself, ensuring that I provide unbiased, compassionate support throughout our work together.

How do you treat patients that you might not be fond of?
I am here to do the work, not rate clients with an internal likeability index.

Do you only take on patients that you like?
In therapy, it's not about personal preferences. I take on clients based on whether their challenges align with my skills and expertise. If it ever becomes necessary to refer a client elsewhere, it's because we've reached a point where our work together is no longer progressing, or the case falls outside my area of expertise.

Do you decline clients?
Yes. If I cannot take you on as a client, there is a reason for that.

How do you view challenging clients?
I see cases as challenging, not clients.

Have things gone horribly wrong in therapy?
Therapy can have its challenging moments, like when unexpected topics arise or when timing doesn't allow for full exploration of an issue. While these instances might feel awkward or incomplete, they're part

of the therapeutic process, not necessarily indicative of things going 'horribly wrong'.

Would you ask me to see another therapist?
Yes, I may suggest consulting a couples therapist or another specialist if their expertise aligns better with your specific needs and goals. This recommendation is based on ensuring that you receive the most appropriate and effective care for your situation.

Would you refer a client to another therapist?
If I know they can get better treatment, yes!

What if we have two or more sessions and I do not return?
That's absolutely fine, but it would be helpful to understand your decision to not return.

Would you refer a client to another psychologist if you did not like them?
Well, you didn't hire me to be your new best friend! My job is to help you tackle your challenges, not to win a popularity contest. Whether or not I like you is beside the point. What matters is that you like yourself—and if you're having trouble with that, we can definitely work on it together!

How will I know if I have good chemistry with my therapist?

- **You Feel Comfortable:** You can talk openly without fear of judgment, and you feel at ease sharing your thoughts and feelings.

- **You're Engaged:** The sessions feel like a conversation with a wise friend rather than a tedious homework assignment.

- **You Feel Understood:** The psychologist seems to really "get" where you're coming from, and their responses resonate with you.

- **You're Motivated:** You leave sessions feeling motivated and optimistic about your progress and the therapeutic process.

- **You Look Forward to Sessions:** You actually get excited about your next appointment—no, really!

Good chemistry in therapy is less about "clicking" perfectly and more about feeling supported, understood, and inspired to make progress. But having said that, it helps if you gel.

Session Location

Can I have our session in my bathroom?
I do not mind if you need to have a session in the bathtub (without it filled and with clothes on please) because I understand you may need to be at home, the kids are around and perhaps you feel safe there.

Do you mind if we have our session in the car?
Sure but at a speed of 0 mph please.

Do you mind if we have our session in the car?
I hope you are warm enough.

Do you mind if we have our session in the car?
Can you please park?

Do you mind if we have our session in the park?
Can you find a bench to sit on?

Do you mind if we have our session in the park?
If you are carrying your phone in your hand, please make sure that you are in a safe place.

Sorry I have my baby in the pram and we needed to be out of the house.
That's fine. Is this something you would like to discuss?

Do you mind if I breastfeed while we have therapy?
Not unless you really, really have to. But I don't want you to cry over spilled milk either.

Can I bring my chihuahua to therapy?
As long as she likes scratches!

Can my dog Zilly sit on my lap in therapy?
Tell me what you feel when she sits on your lap.

Can I bring my new baby to therapy?
I am happy to sit with you while your baby is sleeping peacefully in the room.

Can I bring my new baby to therapy?
Absolutely! Your baby can be the honorary co-therapist — offering moral support and a few adorable interruptions along the way!

The Virtual Couch:
Shrinking Distances in Psychotherapy

Are you seeing my messy room?
I prefer seeing your real room rather than a generated screen behind you.

Do you look at my background at home and form conclusions?
It is hard not to notice your background online but my focus is always on you and what you are showing me. There is that rare occasion where I can't help myself and may ask you who your fantastic interior designer is.

Do you look me up on-line?
I prefer to get to know you, face to face and I really do not have the luxury of time to troll, stalk or research my clients. All of my effort goes towards helping my clients with and through their challenges, in therapy.

Do your clients cry online?
Funnily enough I see more tears online than face-to-face. This may be because of several factors related to the environment, communication medium, and emotional dynamics:

Increased Sense of Privacy and Safety
- **Physical Distance**: Being physically apart from your therapist may make you feel safer and more secure. This distance can reduce the pressure and vulnerability that often accompany in-person interactions, allowing you to express emotions more freely.

- **Familiar Environment**: You are often in your own home during online therapy, a setting where you may feel more comfortable and less self-conscious. This comfort can facilitate emotional expression, including crying.

Reduced Social Cues and Judgments

- **Lack of Immediate Nonverbal Feedback**: In face-to-face therapy, you might be more attuned to your therapist's body language, facial expressions, and other nonverbal cues, which could lead to self-monitoring and holding back tears. In online therapy, these cues are less prominent, reducing the fear of judgment and encouraging more authentic emotional expression.

- **Controlled Visibility**: You can control what I see online, such as by turning off your camera or looking away. This control can reduce the anxiety about being watched and judged while crying.

Heightened Emotional Intensity

- **Focus on Verbal Communication**: Online therapy often relies more on verbal communication, which can intensify the emotional content of the conversation. Without the distractions of physical presence, you may focus more on your feelings and thoughts, leading to a stronger emotional release.

- **Disinhibition Effect**: The semi-anonymous nature of online communication can lead to the "disinhibition effect," where people feel less restrained in expressing their emotions. This can result in a greater likelihood of crying during online sessions.

Therapeutic Focus and Techniques

- **Therapist's Adaptation**: I may use different techniques in online therapy, such as focussing more on deep, reflective questions that can trigger strong emotions. I might also encourage you to express your feelings more openly, knowing that the online format can facilitate this.

- **Reflection Time**: In online therapy, there may be more moments of silence or reflection, giving you time to process their emotions, which can lead to crying.

Reduced Stigma

- **Less Societal Pressure**: In-person settings might come with societal expectations about controlling emotions, especially in public or formal settings like an office. The private nature of online therapy can reduce this pressure, making it easier for you to cry.

These factors combine to create a therapeutic environment in online sessions that can be more conducive to emotional expression, including crying and in the comfort of your old pjs.

Do you also work online?
Remotely.

How do you work online?
Never from a distance.

How do you work online?
You are online. I am online. There is no space between us.

How do you work online?
Safely. I don't byte.

Do you prefer working online?

I enjoy working online with you because I am forced to use all my senses and beyond. I would dare say my 6th sense has spiked since working online.

Navigating the Emotional Landscape of Therapy

Am I allowed to truly express my emotions in therapy?
You are welcome to SHOUT, rage, vent, swear. That's it, get it all out.

Am I allowed to truly express my emotions in therapy?
Go wherever your feelings take you. I've got you.

Are you calm as a therapist?
Yes, because I have a lot of patients (and good humour).

What if I cry?
Go with it. You're just a beautiful human soul, with feelings.

What if I cry?
If you start to cry, try not to stop or be concerned about what I think.

Would my story be too much for you to take?
Not the toughest, saddest, most horrific stories, literally nothing could deter me from staying with you, through the process.

Would my story be too much for you to take?
Nothing you could say will ever scare, upset or phase me. One tends to build resilience over time and my role is to provide a safe place for you to unfold.

Would my story be too much for you to take?
And what would you imagine would happen if it was? And then what would happen? And after that..?

Is my vulnerability bad?
Embrace this moment; it signifies you're prepared to engage deeply here! Being open and vulnerable is essential because it paves the way for genuine exploration and confrontation of your challenges, fostering healing and growth. Without that openness, our work together might only scratch the surface. Vulnerability not only serves as a valve for emotional release but also can lead to a profound sense of relief. Occasionally, I might reveal some of my own relevant experiences to foster a more open dialogue.

How do you view vulnerability in therapy?
Vulnerability is a cornerstone of effective psychological therapy. When you feel safe enough to be vulnerable, you can work through your issues more deeply and authentically. The aim is to facilitate the process by creating a supportive, trustworthy environment and using appropriate techniques to encourage openness.

Appreciate that just like you, everyone has vulnerabilities of their own. Vulnerability is a most basic human trait, one of strength and not weakness.

Confession: I had opened myself up to my own vulnerabilities when writing this book for you.

How do you work with vulnerability?
Facing and expressing vulnerability can help you build emotional resilience, making you more capable of handling life's challenges. It fosters genuine relationships by allowing others to see your true self, which can create deeper bonds and mutual understanding. To work with your vulnerabilities, I employ:

- **<u>Active Listening</u>**: Demonstrating genuine interest and empathy.

- **Validating Emotions**: Acknowledging and normalising the client's feelings.

- **Open-ended Questions**: Encouraging deeper exploration through questions that cannot be answered with a simple yes or no.

- **Reflective Statements**: Mirroring back what you have said to show understanding and encourage further exploration.

I feel vulnerable, will you go easy on me?
You have allowed yourself to be vulnerable here, with me. I promise to be gentle. But do let me know when therapy gets too tough, or if I ask questions you find tough to answer.

I do not feel safe in the world..?
(Please let me not add to that)

I feel vulnerable..?
Do you feel vulnerable here? What can I do to make you feel less so.

I feel vulnerable..?
You have allowed yourself to be vulnerable here, with me. That takes courage.

I could not understand why you made cry so much.
Menopause?

Is it your intention to make people cry?
There is no intention or agenda to make you cry. Crying is just the result of the work you/we do in therapy.

Do you judge me?
I genuinely don't judge. I do not have a double narrative in my head. I just want to get to the 'why' and the 'how'. I am genuinely curious about how you got yourself 'there', wherever 'there' is.

How do you view seriousness and laughter in therapy?
The blend of serious moments with laughter shows us that humour can be a real asset when we're navigating tough spots, especially in therapy when you might not see it coming. A good chuckle can ease tension, give you a different angle on your problems, and make the tough times seem a bit more bearable. Here, you're free to be yourself — go ahead and laugh or get serious as you see fit. It's important to let yourself feel and express whatever comes up.

Is it okay to laugh in therapy?
Laugh if you need to, laugh if it helps, or just laugh it off.

Is it okay to laugh in therapy?
Laughter has well-documented psychological benefits. It can reduce stress, improve mood, enhance social connections, and even boost physical health by releasing endorphins and improving immune function.

Laughing at serious matters doesn't mean you are trivialising them. Instead, it reflects an ability to maintain perspective and resilience. Finding humour in tough situations can foster a sense of control and help you navigate adversity with a lighter heart.

Do you laugh in therapy?
If I laugh while I am with you, I am not laughing at you. And as Niels Bohr said, *"There are some things so serious you have to laugh at them"*.

How do you view humour?
Humour is often used as a defence or coping mechanism to diffuse tension and alleviate stress. Humour allows us to process and confront serious issues without being overwhelmed by their gravity. I tend to use humour in therapy cautiously and only when appropriate.

Do psychologists tell jokes?
No, because the punchline might trigger someone ;-)

Do you have a sense of humour?
If I use humour in therapy, it is never to make fun of or trivialise your problems. It's just my personality coming through ;-0 but yes, I do have a sense of humour.

How do you see humour in therapy?
It is sometimes necessary. There is often wisdom in wit—it can help us see things in new ways or create a sense of relief when things feel overwhelming. Of course, it's always about timing and sensitivity, ensuring that it adds to the therapeutic process rather than detracts from it.

What if I feel I am talking too much about irrelevant things?
When you say that you do not want to discuss your neighbour as he seems to be eating into your time away in therapy, remember that this IS about you. We go wherever you want, even if we have outlined our goals. I am always observing how you engage, function and respond to your world and why/where you place your energies. You can never speak too much in therapy, until of course it is time to stop.

How do you prepare for a session if you know the conversation might be quite heavy?
When anticipating a session that might delve into profound or emotionally charged topics, my preparation involves:

- Reflection on Previous Sessions: For new clients, I will review any notes from initial consultations to ensure continuity and understanding of the client's background.
- Goal Orientation: I focus on the therapeutic objectives set by the client, aligning my approach to facilitate progress towards these goals.
- Research and Study: Should the session's content require it, I engage in further reading or research to enhance my understanding or to bring new insights to the session.
- Mindset: Understanding that therapy is not merely a transactional exchange but a confluence of minds, emotions, and energies, my preparation transcends the conventional agenda-setting of a business meeting. It involves a mental and emotional readiness to engage deeply with the client's experiences.

This approach ensures that the session, while potentially heavy, is approached with the necessary depth and sensitivity to foster meaningful therapeutic work.

Do you feel what I feel?
I see you, I feel you but I will never truly get to experience your pain in the way you did and I will never pretend to know what it felt like, because I don't.

Can you really see though me?
That's the perception people have of therapists but no one can really see though anyone 100%.

Why do I have such an emotional reaction to some of your questions?
Because you have not ventured 'there' before.
Because you are not ready to, "go there".
Because you have a witness to your trauma, pain, loss.
Because therapy can be a little challenging.
Because you feel vulnerable.

Because talking can sometimes stir-up old memories.
Because you feel cornered.
Because you just don't have the answers.

Why do I have such an emotional reaction to some of your questions?
If you have an emotional reaction, we may have hit the truth.

What if I don't agree with what you say?
Yaay!

What if I don't agree with what you say?
About time!

What if I don't agree with what you say?
I am open to being challenged.

What if I don't agree with what you say?
Great, now we can build on something.

What if I don't agree with what you say?
Great! Disagreements are like seasoning—sometimes they make the therapy more flavourful. Let's stir up those ideas and see what we come up with!

How do I handle disagreements with you?
- Express Your Disagreement: It's important to voice your thoughts. Therapy is a dialogue, not a monologue. If something doesn't resonate with you, say so. This can lead to deeper exploration of the issue.
- Seek Clarification: Sometimes, misunderstandings arise from unclear communication. Ask for more explanation or examples to see if the concept makes more sense with further context.
- Reflect on Why You Disagree: Consider what it is about my perspective you find disagreeable. Is it challenging a belief you

hold? Does it touch on a sensitive area? Understanding your reaction can be therapeutic in itself.
- Discuss Different Perspectives: Therapy isn't about the therapist being right; it's about what works for you. Discussing differing views can broaden your understanding or help tailor the therapy to better fit your needs.
- Consider the Source: Remember, therapists are human and can make mistakes or have biases. However, they also bring years of study and experience. Balancing respect for their expertise with your own intuition, is key.
- Evaluate the Relationship: If disagreements are frequent and lead to frustration or a lack of progress, it might be worth discussing how to work through these differences or considering if another therapist might be a better fit.
- Use it as a Learning Opportunity: Disagreement can highlight areas where you're particularly defensive or where deeper issues lie. This can be a goldmine for therapy if approached with openness.
- Set Boundaries: If a topic or approach feels fundamentally wrong for you, it's okay to set boundaries. You can agree to disagree on certain points or ask to approach the topic differently.
- Feedback Loop: Good therapists welcome feedback. They might adjust their approach or explain their reasoning further, which can lead to mutual learning.
- Remember the Goal: The aim of therapy is your well-being and growth. If a particular approach, intervention or interpretation doesn't serve that goal, it's okay to pivot or explore other methods.

Disagreements in therapy isn't a sign of failure; it's often a sign of engagement and active participation in your own healing and growth process. It's about finding what works for you, not just accepting what's offered.

The Secret Life of Therapy:
What Really Happens Behind Closed Doors

How are you, Dr D?
I am happy to share, but I will be eating into your 50 minutes.

How are you, Dr D?
If I act surprised when you ask me that question, it's because my focus is on you. But I appreciate that you ask. Thank you.

How are you, Dr D?
You beat me to it! I wanted to ask *you* how *you* are?

What are we discussing today? I have a plan.
What would it be like for you to just show up to therapy? We know what your therapy goals are.

You do not ask me how I am?
I was taught not to ask a client how they are and this makes sense if they are unwell. I prefer to ask a client how they are feeling.

I am bursting to talk to you. Can I just get to it?
I can see it in your eyes—you're practically bubbling over with something to say. Consider me intrigued!

I am not sure what to say in therapy today?
Say as much or as little as you like. We are not in a rush. Pauses are welcome.

I am not sure what to say in therapy today?
How about we start with, "I'm not sure what to say today, so I guess we'll just wing it and see where my brain decides to take us!"

I am not sure what to say in therapy today?
I see you are having a 'what's on my mind' moment, shall we see where this unscripted journey takes us?

What do you actually do when I am speaking?
When you're talking, I'm not just hearing words; I'm conducting a symphony of observation. I'm tuning into your therapeutic melody, watching for the crescendos in your jaw, the subtle notes in your eyes, and the rhythm of your movements. All the while, I'm composing my response, choosing the right tempo and tone, ensuring our session is both a safe harbour and a thought-provoking journey for your week ahead.

But don't you keep notes?
I do maintain notes initially to capture key insights. After the initial sessions, these notes become ephemeral jottings, disposed of securely post-session. Your privacy is paramount; your full name never graces these pages.

How do I reflect or process my therapy?
Let me think about that question ☺

Reflecting or processing therapy is like thinking about what you have been thinking about. It's about engaging your mind and heart and checking in with what you think and feel, making sense of what was discussed, perhaps finding meaning about those things, looking for connections and if you are able, to draw some conclusions.

Secondly, processing an issue in therapy often means bringing past events or habits into present consciousness and analysing them using our current tools and knowledge, resulting in fresh insight.

I found therapy difficult last week.
Would it be difficult to talk about it today?

I found therapy difficult last week.
I see.. the work has begun.

Therapy is hard.
I am listening.

Therapy is hard.
It is all a process.

Therapy is hard.
Hard…?

Therapy is hard.
It is always a bit tough in the beginning. You take three steps forwards and two steps backwards. We travel therapeutically, at your pace.

Why do I cry the moment I see you, this does not happen with anyone else?
- Because you know this is your safe space.
- Because you have probably been bottling things up for a week.
- Because it is a way to release pent-up emotions and process grief.
- Because my questions may instigate certain emotions.
- Because hormonal fluctuations, particularly those related to the menstrual cycle, pregnancy, or menopause, can make some people more prone to crying.
- Because you anticipate the difficulty and heaviness of the subject matter.
- Because you are not sleeping enough.
- Because you are carrying a lot. It happens to all of us.

Maybe it's because I have that special combination of charm and vulnerability that makes your tear ducts do a double-take!

Why do I cry the moment I see you, this does not happen with anyone else?
Would *you* like to tell me why you cry the moment you see me?

Why do I cry the moment I see you, this does not happen with anyone else?
Does it feel okay to cry?

Can you just tell me what to do?
I cannot.

Can you just tell me what to do?
Let's unpack why you'd like me to make a decision for you.

Can you just tell me what to do?
What do you think may or could happen, if you made your own decision on this matter?

Can you just tell me what to do?
You must try to think for yourself and make your own decisions. I can only guide and discuss the many options with you, as well as to ask you how you feel about each option you may choose.

Can you be more directive?
Can we define what this means and what it means to you? I cannot tell you what to do but we can discuss how you may do it. Whatever the 'it' is.

Could you offer more specific guidance?
Let's clarify what this means and how it resonates with you. While I can't dictate your actions, we can explore possible approaches together and discuss how you might address it.

Can you just tell me what the right answer is?
The key insight here is that there are no inherently wrong answers. Each path offers its own set of experiences, lessons, wisdom, and opportunities for personal growth. Let's focus on addressing any challenges you might have with making mistakes, managing perfectionism, or needing to control outcomes. Sometimes, embracing uncertainty and the space to not have all the answers can lead to the most significant growth.

Can I show you a photo of my husband?
Sure.

Would you ask to see photos of my family or friends?
If I ask to see a photo of your partner, mother, sister, late father it is because it helps me get more of a sense of you, them, your world. You can decline.

Can I read you the text I am going to send my boyfriend?
Sure!

Do you have homework for me?
We're not in skol!

Do you have homework for me?
You inspire me when I see all the efforts you make.

Do you doodle when I talk?
I don't doodle when you talk. I can't draw.

Do you doodle?
That only happens on TV. I can't draw my own hand to save my arm.

Do you ever look at your cell phone while working?
Occasionally, I may check the time on my phone but I always tell my clients when I do pick up my phone to check on information or calendar dates.

What items do you have on your desk?
A cup of tea or a glass of water (always), note pad, a few pens, my phone stand, phone, Mala beads, candles (always lit) and a hand gripper (you may sometimes hear this).

Why are your eyes closed when we speak, sometimes?
I might close my eyes while speaking to help concentrate more deeply on what's being discussed and to tune into the emotional nuances of the conversation. It is a way to foster a more profound connection and presence in the session, allowing me to better empathise and engage with your experience, energetically.

Have you ever been distracted during a session?
I have! Recently, while working in a new space, I saw what looked like a snake's head peeking out from between the sofa cushions. My mind raced—what if it lunged at me? To my relief, it was just a monitor lizard. I tried to track it down during a break but couldn't find it. Later that day, during another session, the lizard made a reappearance, clinging to the drapes right in front of me. All I wanted to do was coax it out, but my client, who was hanging on by a thread, took precedence. So, I focused on drawing her out instead!

It's nearly lunch time, are you thinking about food or me?
It's Client O' Clock time, for as long as I am in clinical practice.

Have you ever fallen asleep during a session?
If my head is down and we are online, I am not napping, just note-taking.

Are you intuitive?
Sometimes I intuitively see visual images when you speak, they are objects, numbers, places or words, I cannot explain these, but they are helpful to me and I may use them as guides in therapy, as I check in with you.

Do you really care about your clients?
I do have deep feelings for clients because I genuinely care about my my work.

What's stays in your mind throughout therapy?
You have placed all your faith in me to help you, and I will do my best to ensure that I do not let you down.

You do not seem to have the answers to my issues.
True, I might not have all the answers, but I do have a knack for asking the right questions. Might it be that the best answers are the ones we uncover <u>together</u>?

You do not seem to have the answers to my issues?
Are we asking the right question?

How do you see me?
Your life's journey, with its myriad choices and behaviours, forms an intricate tapestry; to unravel and understand this sacred puzzle is a journey of enlightenment and profound fulfilment. I endeavour to perceive you with a clarity that pierces the veil of self-perception, to connect with your essence on a profound, empathetic, and compassionate soul level.

How do you really see me?
How do you see you?

Do you see a weak and vulnerable person?
You say you feel vulnerable and weak having to talk to a stranger about your fears. I see a person who has mustered the strength and courage to admit that they need help. But let's talk about how you perceive others, perceiving you.

I am hurt, what goes on in your mind when you see my pain?
For a brief moment, I feel like hurting the person who hurt you.

I am hurt, what goes on in your mind when you see my pain?
Just stay present, D..

I am hurt, what goes on in your mind when you see my pain?
Pain.

Do you get bored of hearing me complain about the same stuff?
You can repeat the same subject matter over and over, and it'll always be new to me. As Heraclitus once said, "No man ever steps in the same river twice: it's not the same river and he's not the same man".

Do you see me as boring, weak and annoying?
I do not see you as boring, weak or a hopeless cause, that's how you see you.

Do you see me as boring, weak and annoying?
I do not see anything, other than two people in the room, trying to understand how to understand the issue at hand.

You must think I am doing all the wrong things.
Do you think you were doing the wrong thing when you signed yourself up to therapy?

You must think I am doing all the wrong things.
Wrong!

You must think I am doing all the wrong things.
You might think I only see your mistakes, but the truth is, in my eyes, you can do no wrong. You're here for support, and that's where our focus should be.

Am I talking too much?
There might be a good reason for that!

Am I talking too much?
Say more about that..

Am I talking too much?
Do you feel you're talking too much?

Am I talking too much?
You can never talk too much in therapy. The space is yours to work with. I may at times, slow you down so we can focus on one thing at a time in therapy.

Am I talking too much?
How are you with sitting in silence?

Am I talking too much, my mind is going everywhere.
Would you like some help with that?

I am talking too much every time!
I see it as a problem if *I* am taking up more space in your therapy.

Can you see the error of my ways?
Do you?

Can you see the error of my ways?
Is there any other way to see it?

Can you see the error of my ways? Can you navigate me out of this mess?
I sometimes see where you might be going wrong but I cannot assume. I will ask you questions to facilitate further insight.

Do you think I am crazy?
Do you think you're crazy?

Do you think I am crazy?
Define crazy.

Do you think I am crazy?
(I think you're crazy to think you're crazy)

Do you think I am crazy?
Is there any other way you'd like to see yourself?

I am not making sense, I am all over the shop. Am I too much for you?
You can go straight, up, down, left, turn, do two rights and I will be right beside you. If I get lost, I will ask (you) for directions. Like life, therapy is a journey.

How do you deal with negative emotions towards a client, Dr. D.?
I do not have negative emotions towards a client. If I do, I look within myself to search for triggers professionally and privately, and will discuss it in Supervision if it persists - there has never been a need to.

Will you know if I withhold information?
You choose what you want and need to share. But the more you tell me, the more I can help.

Do you look at me differently now that you know I have porn binge weekends?
Is that (the porn) something you would you like to work on?

Will you know if I withhold information?
I know there is more to this story that what you're telling me but I am patient and trust that you will tell me in good time.

What goes on in your mind when you do not see me for awhile?
I have not seen you for awhile..

What goes on in your mind when you do not see me for awhile?
I have not seen you in awhile, but here you are, you are alive!

What goes on in your mind when you do not see me for awhile?
I have not seen you in awhile, I hope it wasn't something I said. If it was, please let's work on it.

What goes on in your mind when you do not see me for awhile?
(   )

What goes on in your mind when you do not see me for awhile?
I have not seen you in awhile. Are you putting to use, what we have learned in therapy?

What goes on in your mind when you do not see me for awhile?
I hope you know I am here for you.

What goes on in your mind when you do not see me for awhile?
How long is "awhile"?

What goes on in your mind when you do not see me for awhile?
I have not seen you in awhile, I hope you have not done anything silly.

What goes on in your mind when you do not see me for awhile?
Therapy must be working!

What goes on in your mind when you do not see me for awhile?
You have missed three weeks of therapy, shall I keep holding the space for you?

What were you actually thinking when I missed therapy because I started my new job?
You tell me you did not come to therapy because you found a new job and it was a stressful time. Great, let's use the space to destress!

What was on your mind when I was travelling for a month and did not go to therapy?
Pack me with you, virtually please.

What was on your mind when I was travelling for a month and did not go to therapy?
I wonder what it would be like for you to continue with therapy, regardless of where you were?

What was on your mind when I was travelling for a month and continued with therapy?
Waaa is that the Bermuda Triangle in the background?

What was on your mind when I was travelling for a month and continued with therapy?
I was virtually impressed!

What was on your mind when I was travelling for a month and continued with therapy?
So where were we last?

Do you think I should see another therapist?
Would you like to see another therapist?

Do you ever share anything of yourself in therapy?
Where relevant to our goals, I may.

Tell me, what's really wrong with me?
You tell me you work so hard on yourself, you are tough on yourself. You are doing everything right. You eat well, drink moderately, you are exercising 4 times per week, are big on personal development, listen to podcasts, you work hard and long, yet you feel dissatisfied with life, yourself the world. I wonder what would happen if you didn't try so hard?

Tell me, what's really wrong with me?
Are you asking yourself the right question?

Tell me, what's really wrong with me?
How about we look at what's right with you.

Tell me, what's really wrong with me?
Who/What are you measuring yourself against?

I'm struggling. Help!
I see you struggling, I want to help. You struggle with being helped too.

Are we headed in the right direction?
Wherever it is we are going, that's where we are.

Do you see me like you see your daughter?
No, I do not have a daughter.

Do you see me like you see your daughter?
And what brought this up?

I am afraid you are going to tell me off…
You do not have to accept what I say but I will say it anyway.

I know what you are thinking
Is that what you're thinking?

I know what you are thinking
But what are you feeling?

I know what you are thinking
Have I set a precedence?

I know what you are thinking
You're probably right!

I know what you are thinking
Whoa

"Am I troubling you?"
You are not troubling me, I'd however be troubled if I didn't get to do what I was contracted to do i.e. take the time and the trouble!

"Am I troubling you?"
If I took on the role of a psychologist and called it as my "soul's work", we will need to replace the word "troubling". Can you think of another word?

"Am I upsetting you?"
If you were, what would you do?

"Do you pity me?"
I do not feel pity for you. I just feel you.

"Can I 'laugh out loud'?"
Humour can make a huge difference in therapy both as a tool and as a way of being and approaching life. Some people laugh when they are nervous and some people may laugh because they believe that what they said or did was funny. What matters is that you feel as relaxed as possible in therapy and just feel what you feel.

"Am I distracting you?"
I do not mind if you snack, shisha, smoke or talk to me with a clothes hanger in your hand for 50 minutes. Just not all at once please!

"Am I distracting you?"
Shall we talk about Freud's defence mechanisms?

"Am I distracting you?"
Are you trying to distract me?

"Am I distracting you?"
Are you distracting yourself?

"Am I distracting you?"
What if you put the clothes hanger down for now?

"Am I distracting you?"
How is the clothes hanger helping?

"Am I distracting you?"
Do you want to hang something? Or someone? (Psychodynamic babble)

Is it 50 minutes already???
I know you want to continue talking like old friends, I feel it too.

Is it 50 minutes already?
You are welcome to book in again this week if you see a space available.

Can we talk about my wife and mother? I feel in the middle of it.
(Me too).

Can we talk about my mother and wife? I feel in the middle of it.
What would happen if you took a side?

Why do I keep dreaming about you?
Dreaming about me - your therapist, can be influenced by factors related to the therapeutic process and the nature of the personal relationship we have. Here are some possible reasons to put you to sleep:

- **Processing Emotions and Thoughts**: Therapy often brings up deep emotions, thoughts, and memories. Dreaming about me could be a way for your mind to process these complex feelings or unresolved issues that were discussed during our sessions.

- **Transference**: In therapy, "transference" refers to the phenomenon where patients project feelings they have about significant people in their lives (such as parents, partners, or authority figures) onto their therapist. Dreaming about your therapist could reflect these feelings of attachment, dependency, or even conflict that you might be working through.

- **Therapeutic Relationship**: The therapeutic relationship itself is often an important part of healing. You might dream about me as a representation of trust, guidance, or support, reflecting the bond you may have formed during sessions.

- **Subconscious Problem-Solving**: The brain often uses dreams to work through problems or situations it hasn't fully resolved while awake. If you are grappling with a particular issue in therapy, you might dream about me as part of your subconscious attempt to find clarity or solutions.

- **Reflection of Progress**: Dreams can symbolise personal growth and progress. Dreaming about your therapist could indicate that you are internalising the work done in therapy and that your subconscious is acknowledging your progress.

- **Anxiety or Stress**: If therapy is bringing up challenging or stressful topics, you might dream about me, as a manifestation of your anxiety or concerns about the therapeutic process itself.

In any case, these dreams can be a valuable topic to bring up with me in therapy, as they may provide insights into your inner world and the dynamics of your therapeutic relationship. And it's a good way to lend a voice to the unconscious. Zzzzzzzzzzzzzz

This is silly but I need to talk about cheese.
Cheese, cheesy, cheesed off. I am open to anything you Emmental me about.

Am I supposed to think about my emotions or feel my emotions?
Both. How do you feel about that? Any thoughts?

Why should I care about my feelings?
If you don't care about your feelings, then how do you expect others to care about yours?

How do you feel when I cry?
When you cry, I sometimes cry with you inside. What's inside may transform into gentle pearl drops of wisdom that we share with each other and reflect upon, soberly.

What if my story makes you cry?
When you cry, I sometimes feel myself welling-up too. I may say to you that my mirror neurons are overactive or I am just allowing myself to feel my feelings, like you.

What do you feel when I open up?
You share your truth, I try to see and feel it, energetically. I may not be able to feel exactly what you felt/feel, but I am able to capture the energies that you bring to the space though your personal narrative and respond empha-energetically (a transpersonal psychological approach that corresponds empathetically, energetically and metaphysically to your feelings). I do not look at it from my personal perspective or histories.

Yes but what if my story makes you cry?
I am human too.

What do you feel when I open up?
I try to understand. But I mostly sense you.

What do you feel when I open up?
Should my feelings matter to you, as someone who you contracted to safely hold the space for you?

Do you take me seriously?
I take you seriously. I take everything you say seriously. Seriously.

Am I oversharing?
Tell me more..

Am I oversharing?
No, you are not oversharing. This is your space, share away.

Am I oversharing?
Shall we explore why you feel that way?

Do I make you feel negative?
I cannot feel negative if I choose to be constructive.

Do I make you feel negative?
No, you do not make me feel negative. But I sincerely do not know if the work may be impacting me on a subconscious level. I don't have nightmares.

Can we talk about the dishwasher?
Of course, you can talk about how your wife stacks up the dishes in the machine and how frustrating it is that you have to reorganise it. I am here to listen. But my recommendation stays the same. Just switch off and TURN ON the machine.

Can we still talk about cheese?
Yes, we can talk about how you have to remove all your Tesco cheese when your mother-in-law visits because she comes from a famous French cheese region. My cheesy response would be Edam before she comes!

What's it like to journey into someone's mind?
It feels like I have weekly tickets to travel into your mind for 50 minutes. It's oftentimes annoying because I am forced to ring the bell and get off at the next stop, and have to wait a whole week before I can continue my precious journey with you again.

I feel sorry that you have to keep repeating yourself?
I can say the same things to you in many, many different ways, until you get it! So Eat, Sleep, Therapy, Repeat!

I am not sure what to say in therapy?
Sometimes silence speaks volumes!

I am not sure what to say ..?
Speaking about the trauma can be difficult. Let's just make this space safe for you.

I have nothing much to say today.
I've glad you showed up for yourself.

What shall we talk about today, Dr D?
You tell me.

I have said everything there is to say, now what?
Let's talk.

Am I going too slow for you?
We always go at your pace.

What do you think of me?
What do you think of you?

What do you think of me?
Is there a particular answer you are looking for?

What do you think of me?
You ask me what I really think of you. I *feel* your question.

What do you really, really think of me?
Professionally and objectively…

Do you mind if I am silent?
Take all the time you need (50 minutes).

Why do you put up with me? I start from the positive and always end up being negative.
Because I don't see you, the way you see you. But I am noticing that you're noticing something about yourself. Now that's a great start!

Will I ever change my ways?
People don't change, they evolve.

Am I talking too much?
Keep talking.

Am I talking too much?
Would you like to say more about that?

Am I talking too much?
You can never talk too much in therapy. In fact, you should be talking! I am listening and I am taking it all in and piecing everything together in my mind. I've got you!

Am I talking too much?
It's perfectly fine to use the therapeutic space to off-load. That's what it's there for!

Will you stop me if I am talking too much?
If I do stop you while you are talking it is because I may get a sense that you need a summarisation or a question or we just need to stay with one topic for the duration.

Why do I feel so bad, asking for help?
It takes a lot of courage to get to the point where you have to pick up the phone and ask for help. Do you know anyone who enjoys asking for help?

Am I pressuring you?
There is no pressure when you are doing work you're committed to.

Am I pressuring you?
I wonder what it would be like for you, to just focus on you and not on other people for a change.

ENDINGS

How do endings end in therapy?
Endings in psychological therapy can occur in several ways, each with its own nuances:

- Mutual Agreement: Often, therapy concludes when both you and I agree that the therapeutic goals have been met, or when you feel you have gained sufficient tools/insights to manage on your own. This is ideally how therapy should end, with a sense of accomplishment and readiness for you to complete.

- Time-Limited Therapy: Some forms of therapy, like brief solution-focused therapy, are designed from the outset to be short-term, with a predetermined number of sessions. Here, the ending is built into the structure from the beginning.

- Client-Initiated Termination: You might decide to end therapy for various reasons, such as feeling you've reached a plateau, financial constraints, relocation, or dissatisfaction with the progress or therapist. This can be abrupt or planned.

- Therapist-Initiated Termination: Though less common, I might end therapy if I believe I can no longer effectively help you, if ethical boundaries are crossed, or if I leave the practice. This is handled with care to ensure your needs are considered.

- External Factors: Therapy might end due to external reasons like insurance coverage ending, significant life changes for you, or logistical issues like moving to a different city or country.

- Natural Conclusion: Sometimes, therapy ends naturally when life circumstances change, or when you feel a significant shift in your life that makes ongoing therapy less necessary.

- Intermittent Therapy: Instead of a final ending, some clients and therapists opt for an "open door" policy where therapy sessions might stop for a period but with the understanding that you can return if needed. This approach acknowledges that mental health is an ongoing journey.

- Gradual Tapering: Rather than an abrupt stop, sessions might be spaced out over time, allowing you to adjust to managing without regular therapy while still having support.

What does the process of ending therapy involve?
- Reviewing Progress: Reflecting on what has been achieved during therapy.
- Discussing Future: Planning for how you will handle future challenges without regular sessions.
- Emotional Processing: Addressing feelings about ending therapy, which can range from relief to anxiety or sadness.
- Closure: Ensuring there's a sense of completion, which might involve a final session focused on goodbyes or planning a check-in session in the future.

The way therapy ends can significantly impact your perception of your therapy experience and your future mental health management. Thus, handling endings with care, empathy, and professionalism is crucial.

How did you feel about me leaving therapy?
I was sad to see you leave, because I had gotten used to seeing your face. But your goals were met and so you happily left. I was sad to see you had returned. But happy that you trusted the space and wanted to work again.

How you feel about me coming and going?
You had relationship issues. Over a period of 6 years, you came to see me and then ended therapy after awhile. When you began seeing someone else, you returned for therapy and once more ended our sessions after a period. After which, you started seeing someone new, restarted and ended therapy all over again. I have not seen you in a while. I hope you stayed on with THE ONE.

Therapy is all about YOU, even if there is an US. Yet we are both impacted by the other in so many ways, in and out of the therapeutic space.

You are welcome to come, welcome to go. I am here, until you are ready to unpack and stay.

Why did you not want to continue therapy with me?
I had to let you go because I was not the right therapist for you.

Why did you not want to continue therapy with me?
I had to let you go because I knew someone who could help you better than I could.

Do you find endings difficult?
Sometimes, yes. Because we may have spent significant time together and to not see your familiar face weekly, can feel like something important is missing.

How would you feel if I saw another therapist after working with you for a while?
It can be a good idea to get a sense of how another practitioner may work to resolve the same issues with a different therapeutic approach. You may also decide to try out another therapist for a different issue altogether. What matters is you get the best out of therapy, and you make no compromises when it comes to your mental well-being.

How do we end therapy?
We prepare for our therapeutic ending by winding down and slowing easing from therapy. If you were attending weekly, we would wind down to every other week, monthly and perhaps once every three months. In some instances, we prepare for an ending with two sessions. We have a relationship together, albeit a boundaried one and we prepare for endings because some clients have issues with ending relationships. Some clients prefer to not say goodbye as they fear they may need me again. This is something we can work on. Sometimes we can prepare for endings, have them and it may be the case that you may need to return in a few months. It's all good. There are no fast and hard rules. The end.

How will I know when to end therapy?
When our therapeutic goals are met.

What did you think when I made the decision to end our therapeutic relationship?
I know you struggled to leave your abusive relationship because he was the father of your kids. After some time, and with some strength and strategy, you were able to test your emotional resilience on ending our therapeutic relationship. I knew then, you were ready for new beginnings.

Why might a client break up with his therapist?
Perhaps they just got tired of hearing, "And how does that make you feel?" for the 47th time!

What do you think about when you end with clients?
I have spent a number of years with you, seen you through so many significant milestones. You feel like someone close and dear sometimes.

How do you feel to just listen to me talk and talk and talk?
Honoured.

What do you think about after you have told me something and I have not responded or if I am silent?
I wonder if you have understood my intervention.

What do you think about when I disappear from therapy?
By all means, take a break from therapy. I will not get offended or upset. But like any other relationship, communication and managing my therapeutic expectations helps.

Do you have any thoughts about me and our work together when we end therapy?
Saying goodbye to me your therapist is not saying goodbye to the work you will have to continue doing.

Do you have any thoughts about me and our work together when we end therapy?
When your therapy ends, I see it as your life about to begin.

Do you have any thoughts about me and our work together when we end therapy?
Our therapeutic relationship may end but your relationship with yourself does not.

If we are ending, does it mean I am healed and well?
This may be a goodbye in therapy but it is not goodbye to your therapeutic work, we are all a work in progress.

When would you want to end therapy?
Whenever you're ready to.

Why did you want to end therapy?
I had to let you go because you had continued to not do well. It would have been unethical of me to keep you in therapy.

Why did you want to end therapy?
We were like two ships passing through the night. Two bees in a pod. Two sides of different coins.

Why did you want to end therapy?
Because I did not have the right skills for your needs.
Because we were not a match made in therapeutic heaven.
Because I have done all I can.

Why did you want to end therapy?
You had three sessions. I could see that we were like a ship and rocket heading towards warfare.

How did you feel when I ended therapy after one session?
It is important to find the right psychologist for your mental and emotional health. Go for it!

How did you feel when I ended therapy after a few sessions?
Happy! You are making decisions for yourself.

How did you feel when I ended therapy after a few sessions?
Let's talk about how you felt in therapy so that I may understand your needs or what went wrong or if something worked for you?

How did you feel when I ended therapy after one session?
Goodbye.

Does a therapeutic relationship ever have an end?
Do you have issues with endings?

Does a therapeutic relationship ever have an end?
We work on our endings together.

How will I know when I am ready to leave therapy?
First let's talk about it, to see how you feel.

Are therapeutic endings hard?
It can be, especially if you feel connected to your therapist and more so if they have been with you for a while and throughout your toughest times. But it also doesn't have to be hard. Endings are new beginnings.

Do you keep your clients on longer than they should be, in therapy?
I have no intentions of keeping you in therapy just for the sake of it. I like to position myself as a solutions-focussed practitioner.

Is it okay to see you off and on for therapy?
After we have resolved your issues, you are welcome to return to therapy if something pops up for you, or if you have a life challenge to deal with.

Therapy from the Therapist's Chair: Personal Impact and Professional Insight

What are the positives about the work you do?
I would describe it as mentally stimulating, rewarding, humbling, and a privilege to be connected to that space in your heart, mind and soul. This energises me.

What are the negatives about the work you do?
My inability to take on more clients who need therapy.

Do my problems stay in your mind after therapy?
I do not think of you when I am gardening. I prefer to compartmentalise my digging.

Do my problems stay in your mind after therapy?
Our sessions are about you, not me. You hired me to help you!

Do your clients affect you in some way?
Every patient is different, every problem is different and every session is different. I am not the same person each time.

Does your work with clients impact you in a positive way?
Absolutely, I do feel it enriches my life.

How do you self-care?
I look after myself by listening to what my body needs…meditating or immersing myself in nature and giving myself lots of space.

Do my problems sit with you after our session?
I feel for you and I have feelings for you. But I do not think of you when I am ironing.

Can this client work you do help you in some way?
Client experiences help open up my world. I may take on your recommendation for a play, restaurant, book, film..and for as long as it helps me understand you better and if it sounds fun.

How have you changed during the course of your work with your clients?
In the course of my clinical work, I have added more tools to my psychological toolkit and feel more flexible, open, more understanding with a level of maturity in thinking, that comes with age! The time in practice has also shown me where my strengths are and what areas I excel in.

How have you changed during the course of your work with your clients?
I have become more attentive, a better listener and am able to see red-flags faster than ever. However, because of the nature of the work I do, I am less tolerant in my private relationships for bullshit.

Do you think this work has made you cynical about people?
Not yet.

Is the work you do mentally exhausting?
It is rarely exhausting but I do feel I need some time to be still after a day's therapeutic work and may prefer to sit in silence before I attend to the rest of my day.

Is the work you do heavy?
You ask if the work I do affects me. It does not. I have an out of sight, out of mind, brain. I'm similar in my relationships, which makes me think my brain is perfect for therapeutic work.

Does the work you do impact you in some way?
I do not consciously feel the work I do impacts me negatively but I do not know if it is impacting me in some way unconsciously. I do not ever dream about patients.

Does the work you do impact you in some way?
In every encounter, in every relationship we are all impacted or affected in varying degrees and sometimes we are not even aware of this. It is hard not to be moved in some way by the work I do as there is an exchange of words and energies, a connection and a deep sharing that goes on between us two - every session, every week, every time.

Do you find therapy to be hard work?
I separate my 'work' from home life easily. I don't think about my work until I have to but I do not see therapy as work. Or hard work.

Are you being yourself in therapy?
I can't help it. My personality comes through in my therapeutic work. I make no apologies for it.

Do you think of your own childhood or experiences when a client speaks?
Never. I would hate to miss out on being present with my client if I was looking into my past.

What it feels like to talk to me first thing on a Monday morning?
I am always happy to see your name pop up in my diary the first thing in the morning! Your energy for life is catching!

How did you feel when you could not be there for me, when I needed you?
I wanted to see you again, but I could not. A year had gone by and I was over-booked. It isn't always fair both ways.

What are you thinking when I am crying?
Let it out..

What are you thinking when I am crying?
When you cry, I see you trusting the space.

What are you thinking when I am crying?
Quietly relieved.

What are you thinking when I am crying?
Finally.

How do you feel when I get emotional?
I am always hoping you will stay with your emotion(s) because this means you are not trying to control yourself. You don't need to, in such a space.

What are you thinking when I am crying?
I am feeling too.

How do you protect your energies with all the negative talk?
I do not see clients or patients as taking my energy. From a clinical level, some clients may require more help, more holding but since this is a working space, a loving space, a space where two people want the same by way of the therapeutic goals, our energies should go there. I do however, sage my space regularly, always have a candle burning, set good intentions and afternoon naps.

Do you find this work consuming?
I am always in gratitude to be in a position to hear and help, as it is truly a privilege to be privy to minds and hearts. More often than not I feel sad that someone could have hurt such a beautiful soul and ask myself what lessons you were meant to learn, or how could this experience be

seen in another way, a positive way. I try to remove myself from the equation.

What does someone like Denise feel, to have someone talk AT them?
There are many Denises out there who are trained and experienced psychologists providing a safe and confidential space for you to talk and unfold. You can talk *at* me, talk *to* me, talk *over* me, talk me through it. It's all good. This is after all, talk therapy.

What is it like to listen to someone like me day in and day out, talking about similar things?
Everyone is different. Every story is different. Every pain is different. I may also neglect to remember all the rich details of what we may have shared together, so it always seems new to me. I have a hundred different ways of saying the same thing, in part because I am continuously evolving as a person and as a therapist and I am creative.

Do you treat each client differently?
You have a right to be treated equally, fairly with respect and dignity. When I am with you, you and your world and your challenges are of prime importance to me.

I'm worried about what Denise thinks of me?
My opinion of you should not matter. What should matter is your opinion of you.

How do you listen to clients all day?
When I see a client, I tell myself it's like having a coffee with a close friend.

What do you think about when I cry?
I wish I had magic psychological wand so I could make all your pain go away, however crying can reduce stress and promote a sense of calm by activating the parasympathetic nervous system. Emotional tears

contain higher levels of stress hormones and endorphins, which might explain the cathartic feeling after crying. (Emotional tears have a different chemical composition compared to tears caused by irritants).

Tears can be a non-verbal way to communicate distress, elicit support, and strengthen social bonds. This is particularly true in close relationships where crying can signal vulnerability and a need for comfort.

Can I keep coming to therapy even if my objectives are met?
You can but let's discuss why you think you need you still need to see me.

Other people's problems are more important than mine. Should I come to therapy?
If you keep thinking that way, you WILL have problems. Come to therapy!

Do you get upset when you see me upset?
I don't get upset when you get upset but it would upset me if you did not allow yourself to!

Do you have feelings about me ending therapy?
You abandoned therapy because you have a history of abandonment by your caregivers. You were only trying to take control of a situation against many situations where you felt you had no control in your relationships. You fear being abandoned by me, so you abandoned ship before it could happen to you.

Do you have an issue with me?
Not at all. But it sounds like you've got a running list! Your boss, your boss's wife, your wife, your mother, your mother-in-law, the neighbour, bad drivers, the postman, the guy on the bus, the Uber

driver, the shopkeeper, and even your last three therapists — it's starting to look like they might all be different versions of the same person!

Am I wasting your time?
I have all the time in the world for you. Do you have all the time for you?

What is your opinion of me?
Opinions of other people seem to matter to you. What should matter is how much power you are giving others for how you feel.

What is your opinion of me?
What's more important than my opinion is how much weight you're giving to the opinions of others. What truly matters is reclaiming the power over how you feel and not letting others dictate your self-worth.

When you see me what do you see?
I only see one side of you. The side you feel I need to see.

When you see me what do you see?
I see an individual with a unique set of experiences, emotions, and challenges.

I observe:

- Your Body Language: How you carry yourself, your posture, and gestures which can convey a lot about your current state of mind.
- Your Expressions: The emotions that play across your face, which might reveal feelings of joy, sadness, anxiety, or contemplation.
- Your Words: The stories you tell, the concerns you raise, and the way you express your thoughts, which give insight into your internal world.
- Your Silence: Sometimes, what you don't say or the pauses in your speech can be just as telling as your words.

- Your Patterns: Recurring themes or behaviours that might indicate deeper issues or strengths.

I see you as a complex person, not just a collection of symptoms or problems, but someone with potential for growth, healing, and understanding.

What do you think of me when I am late for our appointments?
I will wait for you up to 15 minutes, but I am glad you show up for yourself, no matter how late you are.

Do I annoy you?
You could not possibly ever annoy me. I am on your side.

You must get sick of trying to help me work this out?
Always remember you hired me to help you. That I will, as long as you help you too.

You must get sick of hearing the same thing repeatedly from me?
I do not get sick of hearing the same topic over and over, it just shows me how much the subject matter at hand, matters to you. So, it matters to me too.

Do you feel negative after our sessions together?
Not at all. I've never felt negative during or after clinical work. Working in mental health is a privilege, and I find it deeply fulfilling to help and support others on their healing journey. It's positive work that I'm passionate about.

Are you ever affected by your work?
I'm mindful of what I allow to impact me and to what extent, but I certainly feel the weight and importance of the work I do.

Do I overshare?
Not in your therapeutic space. This is your time and your space, where you have the freedom to explore whatever is on your mind. Whether you need to dive deep into a topic or simply let your thoughts flow, it's your right to share as much as you'd like. Every detail, big or small, is valuable in helping us understand and work through what you're experiencing.

What happens if you say something I disagree with and want to leave therapy?
If I say something that upsets, offends, or bothers you, don't feel like you have to walk away. Instead, let's see it as an opportunity to address it together, just like in any meaningful relationship. Working through these moments can be a valuable part of the therapeutic process.

Why am I crying?
Perhaps it was just a word.

Why am I crying?
Instead of focusing on the why, allow yourself to stay with your feelings. Feel them fully, dive deep into the experience, and let yourself process without overthinking. Sometimes, the most important part is just letting yourself feel.

Are you upset when I cry first thing in the morning?
What a delight to see your face so early in the morning, even if you cried the whole time.

Am I too complicated for you to help me?
Oh, I thrive on complicated! If you were simple, I'd be out of a job. Let's dive into this labyrinth of yours; I've got my mala beads, map and compass ready!"

I am going all over the place, I am sorry.
Don't be sorry, it is up to the therapist to piece it all together. Go where you need to, I've got you.

Does it ever get too much for you?
I have the ability to create my hours, so if I get a sense that I need a break, I can always ease off on the therapeutic pedal with the number of clients.

What do you think of other therapists?
I have been extremely selective about who I choose to work with for my own mental well-being. This is because the person I work with, has to be more insightful and different in their approach to mine. I am extremely careful about who I trust to help me with my mental health. And so should you!

What do you think of repeat clients?
I hold a positive view regarding clients who return for sessions over the years. This continuity offers several opportunities:
- Longitudinal Insight: It allows me to observe and understand the long-term effects of our previous work together, providing a unique perspective on your growth and development.
- Trust and Rapport: The return of clients underscores the trust they have in the therapeutic process and in our relationship, which is both affirming and crucial for effective therapy.
- Evolution of Care: It's rewarding to see how individuals evolve, adapt, and sometimes face new challenges. This ongoing relationship enables me to tailor my approach more effectively to your current life stage or circumstances.
- Professional Satisfaction: Witnessing this journey provides professional fulfilment, as it reaffirms the impact of our work and the importance of having a consistent therapeutic space.

I welcome these return engagements as they enrich both my practice and the therapeutic experience for my clients.

What's the longest time you have seen a client for?
I've had clients who've returned to me over the years for various issues. The duration of therapy often correlates with the complexity of the problems at hand. It's important to note that if you feel the need for a break from therapy, no therapist should insist you continue against your wishes. Taking a pause in therapy, for any duration or reason, should always be a decision made after open discussion.

How do you self-care as a psychologist?
Well, let's dive into the rhythm of my self-care symphony! Picture this: The clock strikes 3 PM, and just like a superhero hanging up their cape, I put down my pen. No more screen, no more notes – it's time for the real magic to begin!

Drum Roll, please! When I play my Hang drum, it's not just about finding the right rhythm—it's about letting my emotions flow through every beat, channelling my feelings directly into the steel of the handpan. Each note becomes a pulse, each strike a story, as I let my hands speak the language of the drum.

Guitar Hero Mode - Next, I pick up my guitar. Strumming away, I compose tunes that tell stories of my day, my life, or just the wild thoughts in my head.

The Writer's Corner - Music isn't just played; it's written. I craft melodies and lyrics, turning my experiences into something beautiful or just plain silly.

Therapy Time - Yes, even therapists need to talk it out. I have my own sessions, a space where I'm not the one holding the space, but rather, I'm the one being held.

Supervision Sessions - It's like a masterclass where I learn, grow, and sometimes just vent about the complexities of human behaviour.

Fitness Fiesta - I get my heart pumping, whether it's a run, a gym session, or just dancing like no one's watching. It's all about moving the body to free the mind.

Power Naps - Ah, the underestimated art of the power nap. A quick snooze that feels like a mini-vacation, recharging me for the next round of life's adventures.

So, that's my recipe for self-care – a mix of music and creativity, physical activity, and mental health maintenance, all wrapped up in a day that's as much about living as it is about healing.

Gifts, Gratitude, & Graciousness: Navigating the Therapist's Gift Dilemma

Can I give you a gift?
You could argue that gift-giving in therapy is a balancing act of thanks and boundaries. <u>Of Note:</u> Therapists typically don't accept gifts from their clients to maintain clear professional boundaries and avoid any potential conflicts of interest. Accepting gifts can blur the line between the therapeutic relationship and personal interactions, which might affect the objectivity and effectiveness of the therapy. Here are a few reasons why maintaining the gift boundary is important:

- **Objectivity**: Gifts can introduce an element of personal affection or obligation that might have an influence on my objectivity and decision-making.
- **Power Dynamics**: The therapist-client relationship is inherently unequal. Accepting gifts could complicate this dynamic, making it harder to maintain the professional boundary necessary for effective therapy.
- **Consistency**: Not all patients may be able to give gifts, so accepting them could create a sense of inequality or favouritism among patients.
- **Ethical Guidelines**: Many professional organisations have ethical guidelines that advise against accepting gifts to prevent any potential exploitation or misunderstanding.
- **Avoiding Misunderstanding**: Accepting gifts might be misunderstood as favouritisms or could be perceived as a form of payment, which might affect how the therapeutic relationship is viewed.

Therapists aim to keep the focus on the therapeutic process and maintain a professional environment that is fair and respectful to all.

Accepting gifts from clients can be a nuanced issue in therapy, involving ethical considerations, professional boundaries, and the therapeutic relationship.

FYI Here are some guidelines on when and how a therapist might accept gifts:

Cultural Significance: If the gift has cultural significance or is a customary gesture in the client's culture, accepting it might be appropriate as a sign of respect and understanding of their background.

Therapeutic Milestones: Gifts given to mark significant progress or life events (like a graduation, a wedding, or the end of therapy) can be seen as a celebration of the client's journey.

Client's Initiative: If the gift is given spontaneously by the client without any prompting or expectation of reciprocation, it might be more appropriate to accept.

Token of Appreciation: Small, token gifts that are clearly meant as a gesture of gratitude without any underlying motive can be accepted.

End of Therapy: At the termination of therapy, gifts can symbolise closure and gratitude for the therapeutic relationship.

Considerations Before Accepting:

Ethical Guidelines: I will refer to my profession's ethical guidelines. For instance, the British Psychological Society (BPS) or similar bodies in other countries provide rules about gifts.

Therapeutic Relationship: Consider how accepting the gift might affect the therapeutic relationship. Will it blur boundaries or could it be therapeutic?

Client's Intent: Understand your intent. Is the gift given freely, or is there an expectation of favouritism or special treatment?

Value and Nature of the Gift: Expensive or overly personal gifts might be inappropriate. Accepting a homemade card or a small token might be fine, but a large or expensive gift could complicate the relationship.

Discuss in Session: Sometimes, discussing the gift within the therapy session can provide insight into your feelings or motivations, which can be therapeutic in itself.

In summary, while I can accept gifts under certain conditions, it's crucial to consider the implications for our therapeutic relationship, adhere to ethical guidelines, and ensure that accepting or declining the gift does not harm you or the therapy process.

What did you think of the beads?
You went back to Russia and returned with these glassy green beads for me and handed it to me before you ended therapy. It wasn't long before you were hanging around my neck again! Welcome back.

So how did you feel about the flowers I got you?
In the garden of our sessions, where we tilled the soil of your soul,
We unearthed the roots of abandonment, rejection's toll.
With each meeting, progress bloomed, like a flower in spring,
And you, in gratitude, sent a bouquet, a vibrant offering.
I pondered, as I held the stems, so bright and full of cheer,
If to accept or to decline, was the path most sincere.
Would my refusal sting, like a frost upon your bloom,
Or would it teach, in its own way, a lesson in life's room?
I mused on ethics, on boundaries we must keep,
Yet wondered if my therapist's mind was lost in thought too deep.
Should I ask, "What if I said no?" to see your heart's true hue,

Or simply thank you, for the beauty I see in you?
In the end, I chose to speak my truth, simple and kind,
"Thank you for the flowers (draga mea), for the beauty of your mind."

Can I send you flowers?
Can we talk about that?

Can I make you a gift?
A purple framed original poem, written in purple against a backdrop of white was written by you about our therapeutic experience together. I thought it was a nice way to frame it.

What were your thoughts when I brought you a coffee?
Ah, the age-old question of caffeine and therapy. Was it to:
Jolt Us Awake: A mutual agreement that today's session needed an extra kick? Or was it a Peace Offering: "Let's not dive into the deep end today, shall we?" Or maybe a Bribe: "Maybe if I bring coffee, we can skip the tough stuff?"

Thank you, by the way. I guess I've answered my own question. Now, let's sip this like two rebels against the gloom, plotting our next move in the warmth of this room.

How do you deal with compliments about your work?
With gratitude.

How do you deal with compliments about your work?
With humility.

How do you deal with compliments about your work?
I never expect a compliment from a client, so when you say something like, *"you're good, you know?"*, it completely throws me off kilter, especially when I am in mid psych mode.

115

How do you deal with compliments about your work?
You are forgetting that you are doing all the work.

Did you like my boots that much?
I did, so much that I went out and bought a pair several months later, but it would be very strange if I wore them while you were wearing yours!

Do you give lifts to your clients?
I sometimes find it hard to separate my boundaried psychological role and my humanitarian one. I gave you a lift to the station because I had a car, it was pouring outside when you left the practice and you were walking in the rain in the dark.

Did you really like my interior?
Yes, so much that I had to ask who designed it! It is hard not to notice your background, especially if it forms part of your world.

What were you thinking at my wedding?
I witnessed the milestones of your life: your first love, the birth of your first child, and the heartache of losing one who never came home. I stood by you through the sorrow of losing your father, the stress of unpaid bills, the shock of your stolen car, the pain of job loss, and the dark times when you sought solace in alcohol. I was there for the loss of your wife and daughter, the departure of your flat, and the heartbreaking moment when your best friend vanished in Chamonix Mont Blanc. So when, five years later, you asked if I did want to and could I be there on your wedding day, it seemed so natural to say, "I do".

Do you know you saved my life?
You say I saved your life. YOU did, when you saw it was worth saving.

Beyond the Couch:
A Therapist's Journey Through Your Healing

Do you have a practice supervisor?
Currently, I have two supervisors. They keep me in check and I meet with them regularly. Both supervisors have different specialities.

What do you and your supervisor discuss?
You (your identity is never shared though). Me. Our work together.

Do you have a therapist?
Wait! That's still a question about therapy. Yes! I see them when I need to and will get an allotment of sessions for a particular issue.

Do you have a therapist and how many have you had?
Yes, three. Two therapists while I was in training and one that I have worked with for nearly a decade. I trust her implicitly. Anyone I work with must be smarter than me, and be more than me. I am a tough customer and hate it when I am told the obvious. I like a challenging space, but also a loving one.

How do you take care of your own mental health?
I take short breaks, long breaks, nap and I try to work in conducive environments. I have therapy, supervision and meditate.

Will you ever go beyond your remit to help a client, if you could?
I know I can help you beyond the therapeutic space and sometimes I will not hesitate to do so. It is a moral, ethical and judgement call.

Do you ever become friends with your clients?
I have developed connections with a few clients after a significant amount of time has passed (minimum of 6 months) from when therapy was completed. If both parties decide to continue the relationship

outside of the therapeutic context, I would first consult with my supervisor. Additionally, I would ask you to sign an end-of-therapy agreement, and you would need to find another therapist for any future needs.

Why do you have that artwork on your wall?
I am open to discuss the art and the work.

Why do you have that artwork on your wall?
Oh, that? I like to keep my walls as intriguing as my sessions. Plus, it's a great conversation starter! I promise it's not a subliminal message about your inner artist — unless, of course, that's what you see in it!

Do your psychologist friends therapise each other?
Not intentionally, but naturally.

Do you journal?
I journal every day and encourage you to do the same. Journaling enables you to channel, direct and release your emotions in a constructive way. Write or text yourself or even record your thoughts. All good.

Do you dream of your patients?
If I dreamed about a patient, I'd take it to supervision immediately.

Are you an empath?
I am intuitive, perceptive, a sensitive, sometimes psychic and I definitely empathetic.

What do you do with your private time?
That's private!

What do you do with your private time?
Being a psychologist is just one of many hats I wear. I am a writer, composer, singer, musician (I play the guitar and Hang drum badly), business owner, inventor. I have yet to pull a rabbit out of my many hats.

Are you in a relationship?
Friendships, relationships, situationships… I'm in '**Motionships**': A relationship that's in constant motion, evolving and changing, without a fixed definition or end goal and I have many '**Experienceships**': A relationship where the focus is on sharing experiences together, without a strong emphasis on the future or deep commitment.

Can I just say ask you more thing?
Can it wait until next week?

Beliefs

You do not know everything about yourself.

Beliefs act as filters through which we interpret our experiences. If we believe that the world is a hostile place, we are more likely to notice and remember events that confirm this belief, reinforcing our subjective experience.

Are you still using old beliefs for the present?

Keep asking, "who told me that"? "How did I draw that conclusion?".

Are your old beliefs still applicable for the person you are today?

Do you really believe everything your brain tells you?

Do you ever challenge your thoughts?

Do you believe everything you see and hear?

Do you tend to gravitate towards people who treat you a certain way, just so you can validate a belief you have of yourself or that you deserve?

Are you normalising certain behaviours because you have been in it for too long and can no longer be objective?

There is the tendency to search for, interpret, and remember information that confirms a person's preconceptions. This bias can lead to subjective interpretations of experiences, reinforcing your existing beliefs.

We see(k) in people what we see(k) in ourselves.

How would you like to see yourself in 5 years?

Why are you worrying about the future so much, when it hasn't happened yet?

If you spend all your time stressing about tomorrow, you'll miss out on how well today's going.

The future's a mystery, so why let it spoil the present? Save the worry for when you actually get there.

Patterns

What are the patterns you keep on repeating?

Are you choosing partners that resemble your parents?

What schemas/archetypes do you have, that make you choose the same type of partners?

Is your partner really like your mum/dad?

Are you using your familiar past to predict your future?

How do your past experiences influence current behaviour?

Constantly replaying scenarios or imagining worst-case outcomes can lead to anxiety and indecision. Make a decision to be aware when you are ruminating and replay a version of the you, you'd like to see and experience!

Maybe you're holding onto that painful memory because, deep down, you feel that letting it go means losing the part of your identity that led to your success.

Your childhood may have shaped your beliefs and behaviour, but it's your memories that keep replaying the hurt and delaying your healing.

The present

If life throws you lemons, throw it back.

When you are on vacation, remind yourself you are on vacation or else you'll go on automatic- stress.

What cues from your troubled past, trigger you in the present day?

You keep yourself busy because you don't know what to do with yourself.

You need to ground yourself; you are projecting yourself too far into the future.

Are you making new memories?

Why worry about the future when you can trip over the present?

The future

Why worry about the future? It's like paying interest on a loan you haven't even taken out yet.

What would you like to experience for yourself in the next few years?

Things I Say So Often
They're Probably on a T-Shirt Somewhere

Your history

If your grandmother can't make it, it's probably not good for you.

Your parents cannot be blamed for everything. Blame their parents!

Rather than get upset at your old parents for behaving the way they do, why not try to understand who they are becoming now in their older years?

Keep asking yourself, "where does this feeling come from?".

Are you really the same person as you were five years ago?

Five years of growth, but your reactions are still running on autopilot! Time to catch up with yourself.

Whose voice is that in your head, is it yours or your dad's/mum's?

What would you say to your younger self, now that you know what you know?

How has your childhood affected you?

Remember that your parents are aging and you cannot expect for them to behave in the same old ways, as they are evolving.

Emotions & Feelings

Are you truly listening to your emotional tones?

Might you be using old feelings to interpret a new situation?

Can you use your anxiety, as a way to motivate youself? How?
Do you tend to make emotional decisions?

If you don't take your feelings into account, then how can someone else?

Worrying is like a rocking chair, it doesn't get you anywhere.

Just feel your emotions.

You feel fear because you 'fear the fear', rather more than the thing itself.

Are you lonely or just bored?

Our current emotional state can significantly impact how we perceive an event. For instance, if someone is feeling anxious, they might perceive neutral situations as threatening.

Don't stop yourself from crying, wherever you are.

It is okay to feel your feelings.

Thinking

No one really knows what you're thinking.

How many of your thoughts are automatic?
Do you spend your time thinking about what others think of you? Do you think they spend as much time thinking about you?

If your mind goes to the same thing over and over, what are you actually doing to solve it?

You bed is for sex and sleeping. Not work, or thinking.

If your mind goes to the same thing over and over, it'll toss your body over and over while you're trying to sleep.

Do you think about what you're thinking?

Are you so focused on looking for red flags that you've forgotten to consciously engage your mind and remember to appreciate the green ones?

You have many what-if scenarios. What if you just stopped thinking that way now?

If you are going to use your 'what-ifs', in a negative way, why not use your what-ifs in a positive way too? Why choose one and not the other?

Have all the fears you thought of actually materialised?

Everyone has unique cognitive biases that influence how they interpret events. These biases are shaped by individual experiences, culture, education, and personal history.

The idea that we create what we think and see what we believe underscores the subjective nature of human experience.

What we think can directly affect how we perceive the world.

It's time to think about what you're thinking.

Self-worth & Judgement

Seeking approval from others leaves you vulnerable to manipulation and undermines your self-worth. Start validating yourself by paying attention to your self-talk.

What makes you put others above or ahead of yourself?

Long after the bullies bullied you, you are continuing to bully yourself.

Have you actually listened to how you speak about yourself?

Could what is attracting you in a person be something that you need to give yourself?

No one judges you more than you judge yourself.

Have you rewarded yourself recently?

Are you kind to yourself?

What does kindness to the self, look and feel like?

Do you seek validation from others? What would happen if they were no longer there to validate you?

What does validating yourself look and feel like?

Are the things you say to others, really about you?

Are the faults you find in others really about you?

What strategies do you use when you cannot confront a situation or someone?

You find it hard to accept compliments because you feel people want something from you, or they are lying.

You find it hard to accept compliments because you feel you have to try harder.

Feeling like a fraud is useful because it can motivate you to try harder.

If you look in the mirror and shatter the glass, each shard reflects a piece of you. Now, look at your friends—they're all like those shards, each one reflecting a part of who you are.

You find it hard to accept compliments because you only see the negative things about yourself.

Keep challenging yourself.

Just when you think you know everything about yourself, you will learn something else.

If you find it hard to leave, it is because you have put greater value into the other person than yourself.

Expectations

Expectations about others can influence how you treat them, which in turn can shape your behaviour to conform to those expectations.

Communication

Intentions and interpretations. Two critical aspects of miscommunication.

Get faster at trying to catch yourself when you say something untoward, and act on it in the present moment.

Understanding the dynamic between intentions and interpretations is crucial for effective communication, as it helps you navigate potential misunderstandings and fosters clearer, more meaningful exchanges.

Relationships

Different people can make you feel different things about yourself.

Over time, we often start to focus more on the differences in our partners because we get used to the qualities we initially fell for. It's important to regularly reflect on what attracted you to them initially.

Our brains are trained to spot anomalies and differences so that we can keep ourselves safe. It's an age-old mechanism that needs to be challenged often.

When you start feeling resentful towards your partner, it's a sign that something fundamental in your relationship needs attention.

Don't expect your partner to change, understand how their brains are wired.

All relationships require work but it should not be hard work.

Everyone is slightly wrong for you, so choose what kind of wrongness you are willing to negotiate with.

In romantic relationships, love can feel conditional, with expectations like sharing chores. In contrast, love for babies and those with special needs often feels more unconditional, as they depend entirely on you without reciprocation. Recognise that while expectations shape love in different relationships, the underlying emotions and commitments can vary.

People can make you feel things about yourself that you don't know existed.

Choose a partner who is able to communicate and negotiate.

Choose a partner who complements you, not completes you.

Miscommunication often arises when there is a disconnect between intentions and interpretations.

Avoid leaving unresolved issues with your father, as it can be psychologically challenging to navigate those conflicts while marrying someone like him and becoming like him yourself.

Perspective & Reframing

The beauty of the view is where you sit. Remind yourself that where you are is where you need to be, and you need to truly take note of your strength position.

Just because a situation seems similar to you, does not mean you have to apply the same strategies. That may be the older version of you that you are <u>automatically</u> using to apply to present day situation.

How is this situation really helping you?

Is there any other way to think about this situation? Try reframing it.

You seem to be looking at yourself for an explanation, how about looking at the other person instead?

Remember, you get to interview the interviewer too.

Could it be that it is not all about you?

What makes you choose one thing over the other? Familiarity, safety, fear?

If you have a taken up a view of something, has it become a blanketed view for everything else that may seem similar to you?

What maintains the problem? Is it the way you see it?

If you can't change the environment then change the way you see it.

If you can't change the situation, change the way you think about it.

Could the problem with the problem be how you are seeing the problem?

If life throws you lemons, make lemonade—and then find someone whose life gave them vodka and have a party!

Procrastination

Could it be that you feel tired and need to sleep because then you wouldn't have to do the piece of work/project that may make you feel incompetent or unsuccessful?

Could it be that you procrastinate because you're afraid of the outcome?

If you don't show up for yourself, how can you expect others to show up for you?

Do you help people and go out of you way for them because you can't help yourself?

Sometimes just getting out of bed is a success!

Decision-making

Whatever decision you made, was the right decision you made (for yourself) at the time.

What would happen if you let someone else do it for a change?

Do you stay in an unhealthy situation because it seems harder to think about what to do next?

You always have choices. It's also a choice not to do anything about it.

If you're old enough to blame, you're old enough to be accountable for your actions.

Are your choices and decisions all about keeping you safe?

Problem-solving

Don't let unresolved issues linger too long; they can become exaggerated and seem more significant than they actually are.

If it's not your monkey, get out of the zoo (Thanks mum!)

Go by the rule of three. If you've told them once, and told them twice and you have to tell them a third time then it's time to make some tough decisions.

Sometimes just noticing things about yourself is enough to make a change.

Awareness is the start of all positive change.

The more difficult it is, the more you learn.

If you rely on someone too much, you'll never learn what it's like to rely on you.

Sometimes you just have to watch the person you love, fall. If you keep on helping them, they may never learn the skills to help themselves.

Trust your intuition, it speaks volumes. Turn it up!

There is no problem. It is how you both interpreted the situation differently.

There are no mistakes, just experiences.

Making changes

Sometimes courage is just showing up (for yourself).

Try to observe yourself, that's how you get to know yourself best.

What kind of small changes could you make that will make a difference to your life?

What is the one thing you find yourself saying to yourself? How is that helping you?

We don't change, we evolve.

Are you looking at the past and the future and are not seeing the present?

What do you need to start, to stop and to change?

What would it be like for you to make contracts with yourself?

When starting a new habit, consider building it on top of an existing one. For example, if you want to begin meditating, try doing it right after your established habit of drinking a glass of water each morning.

The value of making that change has to be greater than the cost of not making it.

If you don't change the situation, the universe will do it for you. And you may not like the outcome.

You're fixating on the small black dot on the paper. Give yourself the chance to appreciate the entirety of the white space around it.

Body

Are you really listening to what your body feels?

Is it possible that others see you very differently to how you see yourself?

If you find it difficult to look at yourself in the mirror, start by focusing on the top of your head and gradually work your way down.

Could it be possible that you are focussing on one area so much that you can no longer see it for how it actually is?

All your senses have outlets, allow them to flow.

They can hurt you, beat you and destroy you but they can never destroy or take away the essence of what makes you.

Your body is just your carriage. The essence of you is the energy that drives it.

You are both of the material body and the non-material essence of a person. You are soulful.

Energies & Frequencies

It is ok to let someone go if they no longer vibrate at the same frequencies as you do.

When you change energetically, don't be surprised when your old friends no longer align with you.

We're sometimes too small to see the bigger picture.
There is no space between us, thinking makes it so.

There are no differences between us, we just think differently.

Aligning your vibrational frequency with higher, positive energies (like love, compassion, and peace) can lead to spiritual growth, inner peace, and a deeper connection with the universe.

Like attracts like. Light attracts light.

Practices like meditation, sound healing, and mindfulness can help raise your vibrational frequency, promoting physical, emotional, and spiritual healing. The psychological benefits derived from these practices are well-documented and supported by research.

Nature & Nurture

Nature is available to you at no cost, 24 hours a day. It is a reliable therapist to nurture the soul.

Grow roots, stay grounded. This is how you can fly.

The universe will give you what you need, not always what you want.

The brain's ability to change and adapt throughout life in response to experience, indicating that while genetics set the stage, experiences can significantly alter the script.

The connection to nature, known as "biophilia," suggests that humans have an innate tendency to seek connections with nature, which can lead to a deeper sense of peace and fulfilment. What seeds are you planting for yourself?

Death

Think of death as the ultimate therapy session in the grand psychological practice of life. It's that final, firm reminder to make every moment meaningful, to see magic in the mundane, and to extract every bit of insight from your journey before the curtain falls.

*"Everyone should have a happy ending, if they are not happy,
it is not the end"* - Dalia J.

*With heartfelt gratitude to Debra Ong,
whose boundless creativity brings beauty to everything she touches,
and whose unwavering support means the world to me.*

*Deep thanks also to Ben Law
for capturing the essence of the author in her cheekiness
through his photography.*

Printed in Great Britain
by Amazon